The HISTORY *and* HAUNTING STORIES *of* Fredericksburg Virginia

Helen R. Marler

HERITAGE BOOKS
2008

HERITAGE BOOKS
AN IMPRINT OF HERITAGE BOOKS, INC.

Books, CDs, and more—Worldwide

For our listing of thousands of titles see our website at
www.HeritageBooks.com

Published 2008 by
HERITAGE BOOKS, INC.
Publishing Division
100 Railroad Ave. #104
Westminster, Maryland 21157

Copyright © 2008 Helen R. Marler

Other books by the author:
1850 Census of Johnston County, North Carolina

All rights reserved. No part of this book may be reproduced or transmitted in any form or by any means, electronic or mechanical, including photocopying, recording or by any information storage and retrieval system without written permission from the author, except for the inclusion of brief quotations in a review.

International Standard Book Numbers
Paperbound: 978-0-7884-4576-7
Clothbound: 978-0-7884-7463-7

Introduction

In 1993, The Living History Company began re-creating the real soldiers and civilians from the city's past with the stated goal of teaching history in a unique and memorable way. One of the most popular venues was The Phantoms of Fredericksburg; *where we would tell the history of a building and why it could be haunted. The walk took on a life of its own, we never made any guarantees that ghostly things would happen nevertheless some nights we would experience events: shoe laces coming untied, lights coming on, alarms unexpectedly going off, additional footsteps joining us, or we might smell the odor of tobacco or sulphur. The most persistent odor was the overpowering strong smell of flowers that would follow us - sometimes weaving in and out of the crowd.*

People have asked me for years to publish the walk, but I declined, for I was unsure of how well the story would tell in printed form versus weaving the magic by inflection and resonance as in story telling.

By virtue of being in a written form, we are able to share the pictures from our walk. We have used a computer to scan the pictures; and in some cases, clarified a ghostly image, nevertheless, we have not added to or altered these images in any form.

You also now have the ability to revisit the history for repeated pleasure; and we can give our stories more depth and detail. We are also able to discuss, and enter places that we did not have the ability to include on our walk.

Let us begin our journey in time---

An Overview of the Town's History

When the House of Burgesses founded the City of Fredericksburg in 1728, the British paid five-hundred dollars for fifty acres of land. Whereas George the Second was the current King of England, they named the town for his son Frederick, The Prince of Wales. The citizens of England loved Frederick; conversely, his parents hated him.

Frederick married Augusta in a ceremony that featured music composed by George Frederick Handel. Frederick and his parents were definitely of different opinions on politics and finances. They were constantly publicly disagreeing over issues.

One of the issues between Frederick and his parents concerned Robert Walpole, the chief advisor to George the Second. George the First had also disliked Robert Walpole and tried to have him removed, Caroline, the wife of George the Second protected Robert Walpole.

When Frederick moved his family to Leicester, the separation provided the illusion of peace. Once in Leicester, Frederick gathered his supporters, and deposed Robert Walpole from his powerful position. Soon thereafter Frederick was severely injured when a tennis ball struck him in the right eye; resulting in a fatal aneurism.

The night Frederick died, his father was playing cards. Upon hearing the news, George the Second replied: "Oh well" and kept on playing - there was a rock in the tennis ball – they had murdered him.

Within the next fifty years, our country was in a state of revolution and Fredericksburg was known as a hot bed for treason and sedition. The town experienced Revolutionary War skirmishes and even hosted a Revolutionary War Hospital.

In the 19th century, the town experienced four battles and seven occupations. Every time it served a link for ambulance trains. Charles Chewning of the Ninth

Virginia Cavalry was wounded in Manassas, Virginia and brought by wagon from Manassas, to Gainesville, to Fredericksburg for surgery; a distance of approximately fifty miles.

During the Battle of the Wilderness, seventeen miles west of town the wounded Union soldiers were thrown into wagons without springs. The ambulance wagons formed a train extending down the Plank Road from the battle site to Fredericksburg, which lasted all night long. Every time a wagon hit a spot where a plank was missing you could hear the men groan in pain.

The wounded were brought into the town and thrown onto the grass to await surgery. It started to rain and they are moved inside for surgery. The method of surgery was amputation. The reason for this is the lead bullet of the 19th century.

Lead is a soft metal, and when it impacts on anything it changes shape. A lead bullet enters the body and changes shape - as it passes through it will shatter bones, in twenty-seven places; and will tear up all the muscles, ligaments, and blood vessels in its path. The surgeon has no other recourse than to amputate - he cannot reconstruct. If you were to be struck with a lead bullet today, they would still have to amputate; even modern medicine cannot reconstruct from the damage of these wounds.

Even if the surgeon has chloroform, the soldier is afraid to use it, because it puts him to sleep and he might not wake up. As a substitute for chloroform, the surgeon would say: "I'm sorry son you will have to bite the bullet;" and he handed you a bullet, or a belt to bite on while he amputated your arm and/or leg. The surgeon becomes so skillful, he can saw off an arm or a leg in forty-five seconds; wipe the blade, and go to the next patient. Forty-five seconds of sheer agony - this is why many wounded soldiers will walk home, without ever seeing a surgeon.

You need to be aware that the youngest boy to serve in the War Between the States was eight years of age; the youngest to be wounded was ten. There was a thirteen year old serving here in the Battle of Fredericksburg with the Union Army. In the Masonic Cemetery is the grave of the man who served as a fourteen-year-old General in the Revolution.

In both the 18th and 19th centuries, we have women dressing as men and serving with the troops, as well as the women who openly support the military as camp followers, nurses and female blockade runners.

St. George's Cemetery
905 Princess Anne Street

When the House of Burgesses established the town in 1728 they designated that St. George's Parish was to have two lots, one for the church, and one for the cemetery. The present church and cemetery occupy only one of the original lots. [12]

---

[1] A Brief History of St. George's Church
[2] Postcard Copyright R.A. Kishpaugh, Fredericksburg, VA. Genuine Curteich – Chicago "C.T. American Art" Post Card (Reg. U.S. Pat. Off.

Church expansion began in 1849, with the removal of a few graves leaving the majority of graves still lying under the new wing. How would you like to be sleeping and have someone build over you? People have reported seeing figures in white walking back and forth in the cemetery both during the day and in the night.

The cemetery gate seems to have a will of its own ~ close the gate and it will swing open, open the gate and it will swing closed.

As you walk through the gate and down the path you will see a door that leads to the church offices. When the staff closes the church office on a Friday night everything is in order. Often when they return the next Monday morning everything is rearranged because someone does not like for them to take off for the weekend.

If you travel down the hill, next to the church in the far right corner you will find the tomb of John Dandridge who died in 1756[3]. His daughter Martha Dandridge married Parke Custis. When Mr. Custis died Martha Dandridge Custis married George Washington.

The inscription on his grave reads: "Here lies interred the Body of Colonel John Dandridge of New Kent County who departed this life the 31st day of August 1756, Aged 56 years."[4]

To the left of the gate is a large granite stone; marking the grave of William Paul, a tailor in the town. "The

---

[3] Burials in St. George's Cemetery
[4] Burials in St. George's Cemetery

original tombstone for William Paul is encased in a granite stone, on the back of which, is inscribed: "Restored 23 September 1930 by Admirers of Commodore John Paul Jones U.S.N. By whom this stone was first set in place in memory of William his older Brother."[5] [6]

When William Paul died in 1774[7] his younger brother, John Paul Jones, came to settle his estate. In the 18th century the tailor was supplied the necessary cloth by his customers, so upon his death, his clientele came to the shop to claim their possessions.

There is a story that recounts an event that took place during this time. John Paul Jones was in the shop meeting the customers as they picked up their material. The Berry family sent their younger son to the shop and he introduced Mr. Jones to the rest of the family. The oldest Berry son would become the ship's physician for Admiral Jones.[8]

This picture, showing small orbs, was taken to the right of the cemetery gate.[9]

---

[5] Burials in St. George's Cemetery
[6] Vintage Postcard containing no credit or copyright
[7] Burials in St. George's Cemetery
[8] Picture from a postcard with no copyright information. The text on the front reads "Grave of Wm. Paul Jones, Fredericksburg, Va."
[9] Picture Taken by Daphne Flynn October 2004

This picture, to the right of the cemetery gate, shows a cloud figure on the left.[10]

This picture is of the right side of the cemetery gate showing small orbs and a white form in the upper left side. In addition to the orbs many people see two faces in the second full square of fencing from the left. There is the face of a lady on the right side of the "arrow"; and the face of a man on the left side of the "arrow"[11]

---

[10] Picture Taken by Teresa and Sara Auth October 2005

We have enlarged the second section from the left to help you, see if you can find the lady on the right, and the man on the left side of the "arrow".

In this picture, the church sign in the cemetery is to the right. There are orbs, and figures, forming in several places.[12]

---

[11] Picture Taken by Daphne Flynn October 2004
[12] Picture Taken by Daphne Flynn October 2004

This picture of the graves to right of the gate shows a white haze interspersed with bright white spots.[13]

There are several orbs in this picture.[14]

---

[13] Picture Taken by Nick Ierardi, November 2001
[14] Picture Taken by Joani Aveni May 2006

Teresa Auth's family was surprised to find she had taken a photograph of two ghostly images. They found the figure of a lady on the right side of this photograph. Even more startling to them was the appearance of their daughter's name written between the two fence railings on the left at the top of the picture.[15]

St George's Church
903 Princess Anne Street[16]

---

[15] Picture Taken by Teresa and Sara Auth, October 2004
[16] One Cent Postage Postcard Published by The American News Company, New York. Lepzig-Berlin. Lepzig-Berlin Dresden, Lithocrome Trademark.

The heritage and history of St. George's Church begins eight years before the city of Fredericksburg; in 1720, when the House of Burgesses, in Williamsburg established the land area designated as "St. George's Parish."

Construction of the first frame building began in 1732 with the members attending services during the nine years of construction.

The congregation paid $11,000 to have the frame building replaced with a brick church in 1815. Thirty-four years later in 1849, the Nave was erected with the side galleries being extended in 1854.

In 2008 St. George's closed its doors for an entire year to undergo a major interior renovation. The following pictures and paragraphs detail the interior before 2008.

Alexander Spotswood, Jr. donated the first bell to St. George's. This bell was replaced in 1788 by a bell which was used until it was damaged by a windstorm.

There is a legend, stating the bell constructed in 1858 was crafted by Julius Hanks, a relative of Abraham Lincoln's mother. During the invasion of the town in 1862 the tower and bell are said to have been struck by artillery almost twenty-five times.

The current bell also serves as a town clock striking the hour and half hour.[17]

St. George's spire with shadowy figures and orbs.[18]

---

[17] A Brief History of St. George's Church

It is our understanding, from current members of the congregation; that there are many ghost stories about the church. We will share of a few of them with you at this time.

The most famous haunting story; takes place before the War Between the States. A proper lady always travels with a gentleman. This particular evening the young lady and gentleman came to choir practice. Upon arriving in the gallery they discovered there were no hymnbooks no candles. The young man left to find the sexton. The young lady looked down from the gallery and noticed there was a woman dressed in white kneeling at the altar. The woman stood up, looked at her, and disappeared.

I like additional witnesses to my stories – and I found one! One day several years ago, two city employees entered St. George's to wind the clock. They climbed the stairs to the bell tower, wound the clock, and descended the stairs. The man in the lead became agitated:

"What is wrong with you?"
"There is a lady in here"
"No, there isn't. You must be mistaken."

They disagreed about the subject all the way down the stairs. When they arrived at the bottom of the stairway, she was standing there – wearing a long white dress and had long black hair.

Finally the second man spoke to her: "May we help you?"

She disappeared.

The police department does not like for the alarm go off in this church because their dogs do not want to enter the building at night.

We would enter the building through a large red arched doors and travel across the beautiful stone floor of the Narthex; toward

---

[18] Picture Taken by Nick Ierardi November 2001

two smaller black arched doors. These doors opened upon the center aisle of the Nave lined with aged box pews and wonderful stained glass windows. [19]

The austere membership of this church included: William Paul (the brother of John Paul Jones); Charles Washington (the brother of George Washington), and Fielding Lewis (who was married to George Washington's only surviving sister, Betty). Charles Washington and Fielding Lewis were vestrymen of the church.[20] These families worshipped here while it was under construction and laid the foundation, not only for this beautiful building but for our nation, and the freedoms we now enjoy.

St. George's Church has experienced several miracles. On July 19th, 1854 a fire damaged the tower and upper parts of the structure. During the War Between the States it was used as a surgery. These original pews from 1849, survived these calamities, with many still bearing the nameplates of their first owners.[21]

The four-piece communion set disappeared in 1862. Slowly one piece at a time, it has been returned. The Sexton of the Church retrieved the first piece, as it was being stolen. The second piece would not be returned until 1866; by the New York Police Department. Three years later in 1869; a resident of Jamestown, New York, returned the third piece. The fourth piece; was purchased by the church in 1931 for $50, from a resident of Massachusetts.[22]

In 1813, the twenty-year old Edward McGuire; who was too young to be ordained as a rector, became the minister of a congregation of fewer than a dozen souls.

The next year he was ordained, and served as rector of the church for forty-five years, until his death in 1858.

---

[19] Picture Taken by Author
[20] A Brief History of St. George's Church
[21] The renovations of 2008-2009 may have removed these pews.
[22] A Brief History of St. George's Church

In the 18th century the church had clear windows. The first set of stained glass windows was placed in 1885, above the altar of the church. In the early 20th century, over a forty year period, the current stained glass windows were placed in the church. Three of the windows are from the Tiffany Studio in New York.

The first set of stained glass windows to grace the church, was "The Ascension of Christ", depicting Christ in the center, with the Apostle Peter on the left, and the Apostle John on the right. The window was crafted in Heidelberg, Germany and was placed in the Chancel, above the altar in 1885, to honor Reverend Mr. Edward McGuire.[23]

During the next forty years, from 1903 to 1943, twelve more stained glass windows would be installed in the Nave and in the Narthex.

The first stained glass window installed in the Nave in 1903, is also the first window from the Chancel on the left, depicting "The Trial of Paul Before Agrippa." [24] [25]

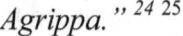

"The Mary Ball Washington Window" was a $1000 gift to the Church from The Daughters of the American Revolution, Mary Washington Chapter. They ordered a design by the Colgate Art Glass Company of New York in 1907 - to depict Deborah pleading with Barak. The window is rendered in medieval style, using small pieces of glass,

---

[23] Picture Taken by Author
[24] A Brief History of St. George's Church
[25] Picture Taken by Author

and is placed on the right side of the church on the Chancel end.[26,27]

During the next two years, in 1908 and 1909, Elizabeth Wallace donated four windows: two in the Narthex; which are shown above,[28] and two in the Nave which are shown below.[29] *"The Wafer"* graces the left side of the Narthex and *"The Incense"* is on the right side of the Narthex. The other two similar windows, are located in the Nave, along the left side nearest the Narthex[30].

---

[26] A Brief History of St. George's Church
[27] Picture Taken by Author
[28] Picture Taken by Author
[29] Picture Taken by Author
[30] A Brief History of St. George's Church

The first of three signed Tiffany Studio windows, has graced the left side of the Nave since 1912 showing; *"Christ on the Road to Emmaus"*. This window is third from the Chancel, and the Narthex, and forms one unit extending from the Nave into the Gallery Level. [31][32]

The second signed Tiffany Studio window was installed two years later in 1914; and resides as the second window from the Chancel, on the right side of the Nave, and is entitled: *"Angel Standing in a Field of Lilies"* [33][34]

The third signed Tiffany Studio window came three years later in 1917. The *"Angel of Victory"* or *"Guardian Angel of Medicine"*, is the fourth window from the Chancel, and second from the Narthex, on the right side of the Nave. [35][36]

---

[31] A Brief History of St. George's Church
[32] Picture Taken by Author
[33] Picture Taken by Author
[34] A Brief History of St. George's Church
[35] A Brief History of St. George's Church
[36] Picture Taken by Author

The *"Resurrection Angel At the Empty Tomb"* shows the events of Easter morning when it is learned that Christ has risen from the dead. This window is the third window from the Chancel, and the Narthex, on the right side of the Nave.[37][38]

The *"Nativity"* is the most recent stained glass window to be presented to the church. Designed in 1943, by Walter Burnam, in a twelfth to thirteenth century style using small pieces of glass; this is the first window from the Narthex on the Right side of the Nave.[39][40]

"Christ with the Little Children" designed by the Colgate Company, at the cost of four to five hundred dollars, was installed in 1907. This window is the second from the Chancel on the left side of the Nave.[41][42]

---

[37] A Brief History of St. George's Church
[38] Picture Taken by Author
[39] A Brief History of St. George's Church
[40] Picture Taken by Author
[41] A Brief History of St. George's Church
[42] Picture Taken by Author.

The best time to view a Tiffany window is on an overcast day because the specially blended colors mixed into the molten glass appear their brightest then.

As we study the *"Angel in The Field of Lilies"* (1914). We are surprised at how the fingers and toes look rounded and almost real. The folds in the clothing are not painted on; they are actually glass that was folded when it was still pliable. The flower petals are made of jagged glass set at angles to make the flowers appear three-dimensional.

"The Angel of Victory or Guardian Angel of Medical Science" (1917) has the darkest appearance of the three perhaps to suggest the subtle presence of ministering angels who come and go without praise or fanfare.

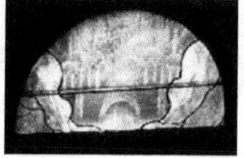

My personal favorite is *"Christ on the Road to Emmaus"* (1912) presenting a single theme from the main floor to the gallery. The best place to view this window from a distance was on the right side of the main floor between *"The Angel in the Field of Lilies"* and *"The Angel of Victory."* From here we could see that in the very top of this window Mr. Tiffany has taken three layers of glass – to allow us the ability to look directly down the streets of Heaven. [43]

After viewing the streets of Heaven in *"Christ on the Road to Emmaus"* we would return to the center aisle and stand by the entry doors. When we looked back along the

---

[43] Pictures Taken By Author

center aisle, we would often find one, or more, of the pew doors had swung open.

The door to the second pew on the right, bearing the number thirty-three, was the one that opened most often. We would experiment with the door by having our guests close it and step back. Many times, the closed pew door, would swing back open. Some evenings the door seemed to "favor" one sex by staying closed for one and opening for the other. We have also had the opposite experience, where the pew door refused to be opened – almost as if it were nailed closed – then as were leaving we would look back and the door had swung open.

A youth group joined us for one of our walks and that evening the door to pew number thirty-three would not stay closed. Several members of the party went into pew thirty-three, sat down, and shut the door. While the door to pew thirty-three stayed closed - the door to pew thirty-five (the pew directly in front of them) swung open.

Here we have pictures of the door to pew thirty-three opening.[44][45]

---

[44] Picture Taken By Daphne Flynn October 2004
[45] Picture Taken By Anonymous Donor

One day, after a wedding ceremony, the church secretary entered the building through the Narthex and proceeded up the center aisle. When she was close to the Chancel all of the pew doors started slamming closed behind her. We have also experienced pew doors swinging open, and slamming closed, as we have walked up the aisle.

This picture contains unique light patterns in the Chancel; some people see a figure on the altar; and the form of a lady on the gallery; by the second column on the left.[46]

---

[46] Picture Taken by Beverly Amberg September 1998

    A unique shape appears next to the left of the cross and some people see a figure seated near the pulpit. The form of a person also appears on the ribbon to the left of the altar.[47]

    This image is below the right gallery with *"The Mary Ball Washington"* window to the left; while the *"Angel in Field of Lilies"* window is blocked by a strange white object which extends a haze over the pews.[48]

---

[47] Picture Taken by Beverly Amberg September 1998
[48] Picture Taken by Teresa and Sara Auth October 2004

This picture shows an "orb" below the right gallery. Some people see a second lighter orb above the arch to left of the light while others see a more distinct figure forming in the same location.[49]

This picture contains many "orbs" above the altar, in the Chancel, and a white figure to the right side of the altar.[50]

---

[49] Picture Taken by Teresa and Sara Auth October 2004
[50] Picture Taken by Teresa and Sara Auth October 2004

This picture is of the right side of the Nave from the Chancel end toward the Narthex. The first window to the left is the *"Angel in Field of Lilies"*, the second window is the *"Resurrection Angel at the Empty Tomb"*, and the third window is the *"Angel of Victory"*.[51]

This picture of the Nave was taken from the Chancel toward the Narthex.[52]

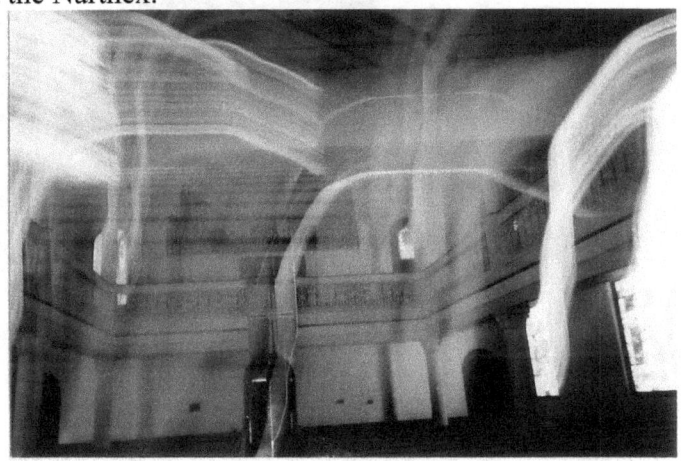

---

[51] Picture Taken by Chris Bloomquist June 2004
[52] Picture Taken by Chris Bloomquist June 2004

The picture to the left shows "two friends sitting at the altar." [53] Above the flag and stained glass window there is a white form along with an orb. On the left in the front there is the form of a figure.

The picture to the right shows many orbs" in the Chancel.[54]

---

[53] Picture Taken by Pat and Doug Wall
[54] Picture Taken by Pat and Doug Wall

There is an orb on the right gallery, and a faint figure in the Chancel, under the center window.[55]

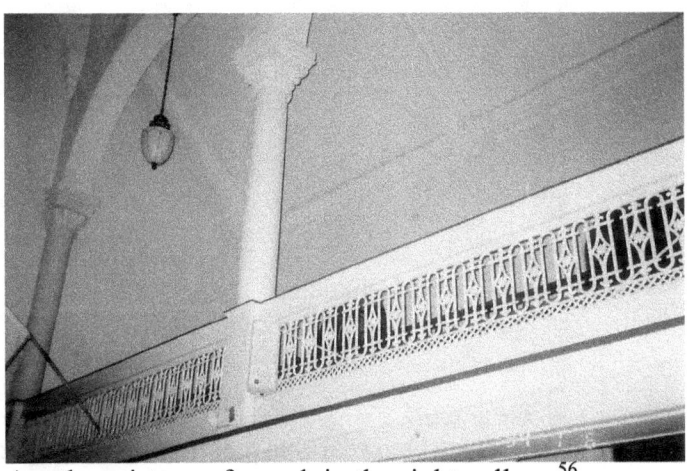

Another picture of an orb in the right gallery [56]

---

[55] Picture Taken by Teresa and Sara Auth October 2005
[56] Picture Taken by Daphne Flynn October 2004

As these people walked toward the Chancel they did not see the "orbs" around the altar[57]

The color version of this picture of pew number thirty-three, has a pink glow spreading from the pew, and extending under the right gallery.[58]

---

[57] Picture Taken by Daphne Flynn October 2004
[58] Picture Taken by Daphne Flynn October 2004

A picture of the Chancel showing more "orbs".[59]

A picture taken of the left gallery containing small "orbs" on the organ pipes and on the flag.[60]

---

[59] Picture Taken by Daphne Flynn October 2004
[60] Picture Taken by Daphne Flynn October 2004

Another view of the left gallery showing small "orbs"[61]

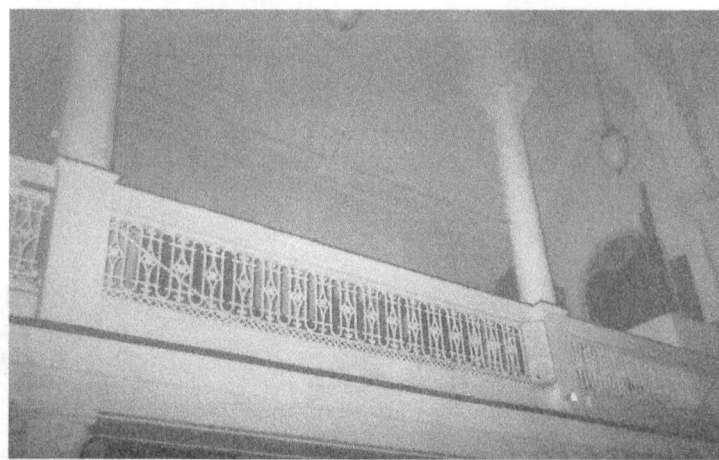

This picture shows more "orbs" and white figures on the left gallery.[62]

---

[61] Picture Taken by Daphne Flynn October 2004
[62] Picture Taken by Daphne Flynn October 2004

Many people see the form of a lady in this picture of the Chancel and gallery to the left[63]

A strange shape was captured on the right of the Chanel in this picture.[64]

---

[63] Picture Taken by Daphne Flynn October 2004
[64] Picture Taken by Joani Aveni May 2006

This picture shows a large orb above the pews and a figure on the column[65]

This picture shows a large orb above the pews[66].

---

[65] Picture Taken by Michael Brown October 2006
[66] Picture Taken by Michael Brown October 2006

There is an orb to the left of the *"Angel in Field of Liles"* window[67]

This picture of the left side of the Nave, shows two orbs to the left of the stained glass window, and mysterious figures on the wall. [68]

---

[67] Picture Taken by Michael Brown October 2006
[68] Picture Taken by Michael Brown October 2006

This picture shows an orb on the left side of the Nave[69]

There are several figures in this picture, of the left side of the Nave, near the Chancel.[70]

---

[69] Picture Taken by Michael Brown October 2006
[70] Picture Taken by Michael Brown October 2006

A picture of the Gallery, toward the Narthex, showing orbs and a bright light[71]

This picture of the left Gallery, shows a distinct "orb", and "large cloud form to the left of the pillar"[72]

---

[71] Picture Taken by Michael Brown October 2006

815 Princess Anne Street[73]

---

[72]Picture Taken by Kimberley Wierzbicki October 2000
[73] Picture is an 1881 stereoptican image in possession of Historic Fredericksburg Foundation, Inc. Published on URL:
http://departments.umw.edu/hipr/www/Fredericksburg/1881pics.htm

The early 20th century post card[74] is of the Smithsonian Castle built on the Mall in Washington DC in 1855 with red sandstone. Compare the postcard image with the one taken in 1881 showing the courthouse in its original red sandstone – do you see a resemblance?

Both buildings were designed by architect James Renwick, Jr. who designed our courthouse in 1854 - at the cost of $14,000. His most famous work was St Patrick's Cathedral in New York. [75]

The Courthouse is haunted – things are rearranged; they disappear; and people hear voices. The courthouse staff calls the ghost Courtney and they wonder why the building would be haunted.

If we study the history of the buildings in the eight and nine hundred blocks of Princess Anne Street; we will learn some reasons why the courthouse could be haunted.

As we have discussed, St. George's Church was a surgery. Next to the church stands the Town Hall one of four Town Halls this old in the country - located in Boston, Charleston, Alexandria, and Fredericksburg.

907 Princess Anne Street[76]

---

[74] Vintage Postcard in Possession of Author
[75] Picture of James Renwick was obtained from the St Patrick's Cathedral Website
[76] Picture Taken by Author

The Town Hall built in 1816 served as the center for town government for 166 years. After the city government moved their offices to another location in1982 the Town Hall became the home of the Fredericksburg Area Museum and Cultural Center.

In the 19th century people visited the market on a daily basis purchasing the necessary supplies for the day's meal. So in addition to government proceedings the Town Hall was the market place.

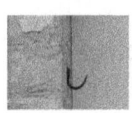 Here people could purchase fresh and preserved produce and meats. The once open archways on the river side of the  building still hold the meat hooks used by the vendors. [77]

The expression "all's fair" comes from the vendors' belief they could be liberal in their weighing of the goods. The merchants became so talented they could add extra weight, in some form, in front of the city employee assigned to monitor their activities.

This picture of the river side of the building shows the original, now enclosed, archways and the market square.[78]

---

[77] Picture Taken by Author
[78] Picture Taken by Author

The Town Hall became the center of social events. We had balls and receptions in this building. When Lafayette visited America he was entertained at this site.

On the south side of the Town Hall, you can still view the original steps used in the early 19th century by dignitaries and citizens. If you pause for a moment you can envision them going about their daily chores.[79]

During the War Between the States the Town Hall became a Federal Hospital at one time there were seventy-five Union Soldiers listed as patients in this building.

Corner of Princess Anne and George Streets[80]

The Farmer's Bank of 1820 [now PNC Bank] still stands on the corner of Princess Anne and George Streets. During the Federal Occupation of the town this was the

---

[79] Picture Taken by Author
[80] Picture Taken by Author

Union Provost Marshall's office. Here they controlled the rate of exchange – telling the people what we could and could not buy. They even told us on which Sundays we could or could not attend church.

When the Union Army entered the building they blew up the safe, only to discover that all the money was gone, and the only thing left were documents which were discarded all over the streets.

On the left corner of this building is the signature of a P.D. Norvill carved into the brick; which may or may not, be the name of a soldier serving in Fredericksburg.

The 19th century soldier had a great fear of being buried in an unknown grave. One method of identification was to take a piece of paper with your name and address and pin this to your coat, or put it inside your coat pocket. Or you could take your belt buckle, carve your name or initials into the metal, and put it back on.

You could place your name on a piece of paper in your coat pocket - nevertheless the greatest clothing supplier of a solider was a dead soldier - your clothing was stolen and your name was gone.

So the soldier could buy or make an ident–i- tag by taking a coin or reshaping a bullet. Then carve your name or initials in the metal. The last step would be to punch a hole in the metal and put it on a string or thong around your neck – the string would break your name was gone.

19th century graffiti is usually name and unit. Could they have left their names in case their loved ones came looking and would then know where to find their bodies?

During the Federal occupation of the town between the battle of Fredericksburg and the Chancellorsville Campaign - Abraham Lincoln came to review the troops.

His son had celebrated his tenth birthday and as a present Mr. Lincoln brought him from Washington DC to the Lacy House so the child could see a rebel. From the Lacy House Mr. Lincoln came into town riding in a carriage drawn by four iron gray horses accompanied by a military band playing music.

The carriage stopped in front of the Farmer's Bank. Mr. Lincoln started to climb out of the carriage but Edwin Stanton and Allen Pinkerton stopped him. He never got out of the carriage and no one came into town to see him.

President Jefferson Davis had previously come to the town and everyone had come to see him. Only two towns can boast being visited by both Presidents Lincoln and Davis – Richmond and Fredericksburg, Virginia.[81]

In December of 1862, during the invasion of the town, Clara Barton was across the river at the Lacy House treating a wounded Confederate soldier - they will send for her.

The Confederate begged her not to go, and she replied that the wounded needed her, and she would go to assist them. As she came up these streets; the man with her became wounded and she received bullet holes in her skirts.

She continued her journey into town to treat the wounded soldiers, from both sides, in St. George's and the Presbyterian Churches.

---

[81] The Yankee Banner, and The Journal of Betty Herndon Maury.

Corner of Princess Anne Street and George Streets[82]

    The Presbyterian Church was built in 1834, less than thirty years later the pews will be made into stretchers and coffins and the bell was melted for the Southern cause.

    The hospital system of the War Between the States is the precursor to the military hospital of today. We had the pre op; the triage; the surgery; the post op. Every journal recounts how every house is lit up; every house is a surgery; there are limbs in every yard, there are bodies everywhere.

    While we could attribute ghostly visits in the court house to the traumas of the invasion and surgery – I have another possibility; let us discuss another reason why the courthouse might be haunted.

---

[82] Hand Colored Postcard Published by W. L. Bond Druggist, Fredericksburg, Va. Post Cards of Quality – The Albertype Co., Brooklyn, N.Y.

815 Princess Anne Street

The original 18th century courthouse on this site was visited by many attorneys, including Patrick Henry, who would make a mark on our history.

The current spire[83] was used by the troops as a signal tower, flying flags by day, and using torches by night, to send messages. You could see the troops responding from the opposite hills.

The bell in this tower was manufactured by The Revere Foundry and was ordered as a special gift for the City of Fredericksburg by Silas Wood of Spotsylvania and New York.[84]

Mr. Renwick designed the courthouse as a one story open building with a cathedral effect so you could see and enjoy the walnut hand carved beams in the vaulted ceiling.

---

[83] Picture Taken by Author
[84] "The Romance Stories of the Past" by Helen R Marler

In the 1940s it was determined that the interior would be more useful if divided into two stories. A drop ceiling was put in place on the new first floor level. If someone destroyed your architectural creation in this manner, what would you do? Perhaps Mr. Renwick is angry with the changes made to his creative work.

This picture of the Courthouse Tower shows the progression of the spire heavenward and also contains mysterious figures and forms.[85]

This picture shows orbs around the North end of the Courthouse.[86]

---

[85] Picture Taken by Joni Aveni May 2006
[86] Picture Taken by Daphne Flynn October 2004

Many cloudy figures appear on the North end of the courthouse in this picture.[87]

Another picture showing orbs and white figures on the North end of the courthouse.[88]

---

[87] Picture Taken by Teresa and Sara Auth October 2005
[88] Picture Taken by Teresa and Sara Auth October 2005

A picture of a white figure by the second floor window to the left of the front door[89]

This picture of the second floor windows, on left side of the spire, shows some of the original hand carved beams and some orbs.[90]

---

[89] Picture Taken by Teresa and Sara Auth October 2004
[90] Picture Taken by Daphne Flynn October 2004

This is a picture of a large orb in the center and smaller orbs in the windows on left side of the second story [91]

A picture of another orb between the same two windows [92]

---

[91] Picture Taken by Daphne Flynn October 2004
[92] Picture Taken by Nick Ierardi November 2001

Here is another picture, from the North end of the Courthouse, with orbs and figures scattered across the image.[93]

802 and 804 Princess Anne Street[94]

---

[93] Picture Taken by Beverly Amberg September 1998
[94] Picture Taken by Author

During the Revolution the Hessian soldiers accused British physician Robert Wellford of treating American Prisoners with too much kindness and compassion. These accusations caused him to be drummed out the British Army. Whereas one of his patients had been the son of Governor Alexander Spotswood, of Virginia, he was able to obtain a letter of recommendation from George Washington.

Dr. Wellford came to Fredericksburg, Virginia and purchased a house, which still stands, on the corner of Pitt and Caroline Streets. The house was known for its beautiful doors.

In the 19th century the house was still owned by the Wellford Family, who were physicians, like their ancestor. When the citizens were warned to leave town in November of 1862 the Wellford Family fled to their country home in Spotsylvania County.

On December 16, 1862 many citizens returned to the town, some walking in knee deep mud, to see what has happened to their possessions.

The Wellford Family found that the Union Army had occupied their home. The house had sustained damage from thirty cannon balls. To stave off the bitterly cold December weather the soldiers had stuffed the holes with material; and had burned the beautiful doors. They also found the china has been smashed, the portraits were ripped from the walls, and the furniture was in pieces.

The Wellford Family returned to their country home to wait out the war.

The next spring the Union and Confederate Armies converged at Chancellorsville, Virginia. The Union Army occupied the Chancellor House, locking the women and children in the basement.

A short distance from the Chancellor Family General Lee and General Jackson had their last meeting. General Jackson took two-thirds of the Confederate Army around the end of the Union Army.

The Confederates were guided by a thirteen year old local boy, whose name is Charlie Wellford. The Wellford Family owned Catherine Furnace where the Battle of Chancellorsville took place. They had moved from one war zone into another.

You may find of interest that the Wellford descendants continued to serve as physicians. One of these Wellford descendants is honored in a stained glass window in Florida for his help in finding a cure for malaria.

The duplex located at 804 Princess Anne Street was built by Dr. Beverly Randolph Wellford in 1826 and may have served as his office. It has since served as shops, apartments and offices. The majority of the tenants have heard the sound of the chiming of a grandfather clock there is no grandfather clock in or near the building.

When it was a shop the owner had a series of bookshelves and tables on the second floor. One morning a small boy and his mother, who were regular customers were waiting outside for the store to open. She unlocked the door and they all entered together. The boy asked if he could go upstairs and look at the books. Permission was granted.

He came right back down and asked: "Who is that man in the funny clothing up stairs reading books?"

He described a man in 18th century clothing sitting on one of the chairs reading a book. Concerned that she might startle the child the owner replied "He is a friend of ours who came in earlier"

Of course when she went upstairs to check on the situation she found no one was there.

The same shop keeper had a personal encounter with a ghost one night when they had been renovating the building. They had spent a long day cleaning and painting and as the evening wore on they sent out for food. That night they had stayed much longer than planned and were so tired that they decided to sleep on the floor.

At about one o'clock, in the morning, they heard someone come in the front door and up the stairs; the sound came closer until a dark figure walked past them.

They spoke with prior tenants, who believed the figure was Dr. Wellford returning home from treating an ill patient late at night.

More recently, the right side of the duplex was the home of a man who insisted the house was not haunted. The only sound he heard was his dog walking up and down the stairs. One day he was reading a book, with the dog lying on the floor beside his chair. Suddenly, he heard the familiar sound of his dog coming down the stair – he soon vacated the house.

This picture shows an orb on the far right side of the building door to the Welford Duplex.[95]

---

[95] Picture Taken by Teresa and Sara Auth October 2005

This picture shows an orb above the duplex and two on the front of the building.[96]

This picture shows an orb a large orb to left and more orbs on the building[97]

---

[96] Picture Taken by Teresa and Sara Auth October 2005
[97] Picture Taken by Daphne Flynn October 2004

Corner of Princess Anne & Hanover Streets[98]

    The early leaders of our town and of our country were members of the Masonic Order. The original Masonic Lodge of Fredericksburg was located nearer to the Rappahannock River.

    On display in the present Masonic Lodge is the Bible which was used at the swearing in of Presidents George Washington and George H.W. Bush. Also on display is an original Peale portrait of George Washington.

    During the invasion of the town the Masonic Lodge was pressed into service as a surgery. One soldier's journal records the great sorrow he feels as he is lying wounded on the floor of the building.

    In his pain he notices the Masonic emblems on the wall and notes how sad it is to see his fellow soldiers lying under the noble symbols in such severe physical pain.

---

[98] Picture Taken by Author

715 Princess Anne Street [99]

In 1982 the town hall was converted to the Fredericksburg Area Cultural Center and Museum and the City Government Offices were relocated to 715 Princess Anne Street. This building was constructed as a Federal Post Office in 1909.

The steps support six white columns and two beautiful lamp posts graced by Griffins[100].

---

[99] Postcard Copyright Post Cards of Quality – The Albertype Co., Brooklyn, N.Y. Publ. by W.L. Bond
[100] Pictures Taken by Author

The exterior of the building hints at the grandeur of the interior with its white arched ceilings detailed with carvings. Our society has, lost so very much, we no longer build our government buildings to be esthetically pleasing.

An early 20th century post card, showing the beautiful interior.[101]

301 and 303 Hanover Street[102]

---

[101] Post Card Containing no copyright or credit
[102] Picture Taken by Author

The early 20th century duplex, on the corner of Hanover and Princess Anne Streets, is believed to be one of the first motor inns in Virginia.

In 1862 this site was the home of Mrs. Maria Daniel. There is a Federal Blockade on the river and we have three recorded blockade runners. One is Matthew Fontaine Maury the "Father of Oceanography"; the other two are women Maria Daniel and her cousin Miss Travers.

Maria had married Mr. Daniel, when she was nineteen, and he was more than three times her age. At the time of her marriage she announced that while she had been born in Pennsylvania she would never associate with the Yankees again.

She was in her home during the invasion of the town where she saw the looting, and the destruction of war firsthand. Maria and her two children were driven from their home and they walked many miles to the Chancellor House in the middle of the night to seek refuge. Her third child will be born a few months later.

Maria, like so many others, returned home as soon as possible. To her door came a woman who was working with Union Army seeking bandages to treat wounded soldiers.

Maria took one look at this woman, who was actually Clara Barton, and said "I saw what your Union Army did to this town. If I had one string left I would burn it before I would give it to you" She was reported to the Provost Marshall for her bad attitude.

The duplex with orbs and cloud figures[103]

308 Hanover Street[104]

In 1802 The Methodist Church became the third religion to have a congregation in Fredericksburg. That year they constructed a small frame church on George Street next to the present-day Hurkamp Park.

---

[103] Picture Taken by Daphne Flynn October 2004
[104] Picture Taken by Chris Bloomquist June 2004. The original of this picture contains a mysterious pink glow.

A few decades later, in 1841, the trustees purchased this large property on Hanover Street where they constructed a simple brick church.

The presence of this church can be credited to The Reverend John Kobler, a retired minister who had joined the congregation, as a layman, in 1821. The people were so fond of John Kobler that they began to refer to him as Father Kobler.

John Kobler died in 1843 soon after the new church was completed and was buried under the pulpit. His wife died in 1855 and was also buried there. [105]

In 1844 The Methodist Episcopal Church went through a terrible divisiveness. In Fredericksburg, on this site, met the membership of Methodist Episcopal Church (sometimes referred to as Methodist Church North) and several blocks over, on the corner of Charles and Lewis Streets, met the membership of The Methodist Church South. [106]

For some unknown reason, during the invasion of the town the Methodist Episcopal Church was severely damaged. There was structural damage and the marble pulpit; the pews and other furnishings were removed.

Whereas the Methodist Church South building was not so damaged, the reunited congregation met there until the current church could be constructed in 1882.

When the members rebuilt the church on this site they lovingly replaced the bodies Father Kobler and his wife Mary side by side under the altar. [107]

The present structure has seventeen stained glass windows honoring members who were special citizens of Fredericksburg.

---

[105] History provided by The Fredericksburg Methodist Church
[106] History provided by The Fredericksburg Methodist Church
[107] "True Love Stories of the Past"

A picture of the Methodist Church with a pink glow[108].

This picture of the Methodist Church has a large and small orb and there is a hint of a figure beginning to form.[109]

---

[108] Picture Taken by Chris Bloomquist June 2004
[109] Picture Taken by Mrs. Cameron Sutton

Corner of Princess Anne and Charlotte Streets [110]

Haydon Hall was built about 1836 as a private home and now serves as an office complex.

I first learned it was haunted when a lady said to me: "I went to Haydon Hall to pick up my sister after work. While I was waiting for her to finish her paper work we heard the sounds of an office reception. Neither of us thought anything of it until we realized that we were the only people in the building."

I visited the building and learned that things get rearranged, things disappear, and they hear a lot of parties going on.

It is believed that the wife killed the husband and she is still there. Therefore I caution men not to push their lady to that point. Ladies I very strongly suggest that you do not yield to the temptation – for she did not solve the problem, she is still there.

---

[110] Picture Taken by Teresa and Sara Auth October 2004

This picture shows orbs on the building and street.[111]

A picture of orbs on the roof and on the left corner[112]

---

[111] Picture Taken by Daphne Flynn October 2004
[112] Picture Taken by Daphne Flynn October 2004

"This is the last picture I took before my camera stopped working...very bright orb with several other orbs."[113]

Denise Bryant experienced something that has occurred repeatedly on our phantom walks in various locations. We would have cameras stop working or the batteries would fall out. There were some evenings when you would aim a camera at a building and it would not work nevertheless if you turned away from the building your camera would work perfectly. We would have cameras automatically rewind, sometimes on the sixth exposure, and digital cameras insist the brand new disc was full.

Sometimes we would have the reverse problem where cameras would not work at places where others had taken pictures and they would work perfectly at the locations where other cameras failed.

---

[113] Picture Taken by Denise Bryant August 2003

Fredericksburg Visitor Center
706 Caroline Street[114]

Do you know what a confectionary is? In the 19th century the confectionary is where we buy our candy, our fruits and our baked goods. Whereas, a good homemaker always insists that she never buys commercial baked goods. The confectioner's profits must come from the sale of fruits and candies.

In addition to the local farmers' fruits in season, the ocean-going vessels on the river bring pineapples and other fruits from distant lands to delight housewives on their daily shopping trips.

The bright, colorful, hard candies displayed in clear jars, are in some cases, also used for medical purposes (i.e. horehound for sore throats).

Chocolate was originally a drink made from the coarse powder of the cocoa bean. During the 18th century Mr. John Baker converted paper mills in Massachusetts into chocolate mills, where the powder was refined for baking.

In 1827, Mr. Baker and his partner, Mr. German, published the first brownie recipe (made with maple syrup).

---

[114] Picture is from a postcard published in the 1970s by Virginia Photo Color Cards, Rt. 2, Box 11-X, Keysville, VA 23947-804-736-8144 McGraw Color Graphics, Kansas City, MO 64108. Photo by Linda Card

Baker's German's Chocolate, actually bears the two surnames of the manufacturers, and is not a nationality.[115]

Charlotte Street is named for the wife of King George II, who had selected her name from a list of suitable partners. The night of their wedding she sang for the guests at their wedding supper. Charlotte remained devoted to George II the rest of her life.

We are now journeying down Charlotte Street toward one of the confectionaries in town. The three story building which now serves as the Fredericksburg Visitor Center, was built by Anthony Cale, with his shop on the first floor and his family residence on the two upper floors.

In 1850 Mr. Cale died and was buried in the Masonic Cemetery, his daughter, Kate, who owned the house next door, made the confectionary into Kate's Confectionary and Toy Shop.

During the Federal occupation of the town Kate's Confectionary became a Detention Center (a jail) where the Union Army held the young men and the elderly men until they could send them to Washington D.C. and Fort Delaware.

It is rumored that there are still three men on the top floor. Recently, a city employee who is a computer technician, was working on the computers on the top floor. He noticed that a little old man kept coming in and out of the room. He wondered who the man was so when he went downstairs on an errand he inquired about this mysterious employee.

"Oh, you have met Sam. He's our ghost".

As he returned to the third floor the computer technician determined he would speak with Samuel. Taking his seat, he began to work with the computer and soon Sam entered the room. This time the technician welcomed Sam

---

[115] Another example of this misconception is German Chocolate Cake – a recipe created in Texas in 1958 named for the main ingredient German's Flour.

who came over to watch the screen and was fascinated by the changing colors. When the technician turned off the monitor, Sam disappeared.

An employee who works on the third floor has noticed that when she leaves her office all of the windows are closed – many times upon her return there is a window pushed open from the bottom.

Some of our guests have seen the blinds moving in the windows or they have seen objects move from window to window. One night some members of a ghost- hunting club saw the building move. The experience was so vivid and clear that the entire group returned to the Visitor Center, before leaving town, and the building repeated the act of movement for them and for others in the group.

A picture of the front of the building with clouds on Caroline Street and many people see a face in the upper right hand corner.[116]

---

[116] Picture Taken by Beverly Amberg September 1998

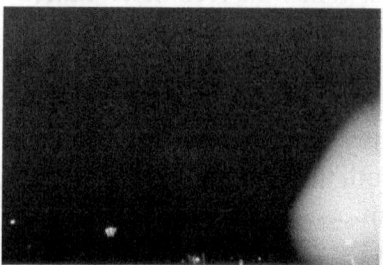

A mysterious blue orb appears on Caroline Street, near the Visitor Center.[117]

The pictures below are of the back of the building and contain large cloud shaped figures, orbs, and in some cases, figures in the windows. [118]

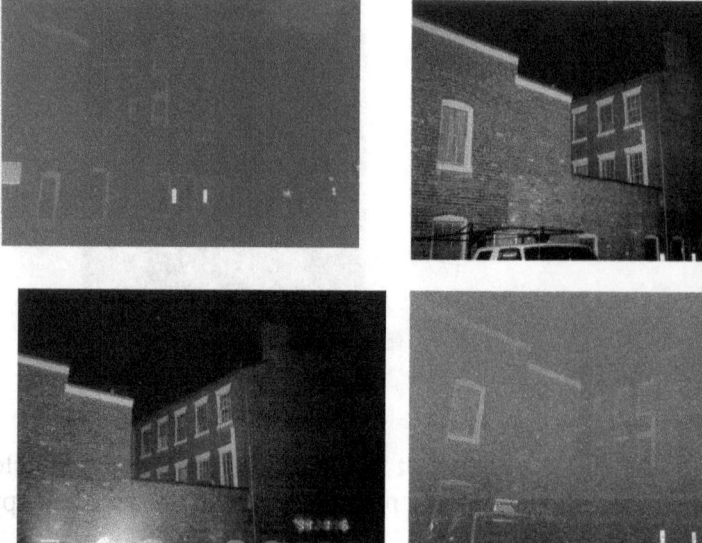

---

[117] Picture Taken by Daphe Flynn October 2004
[118] First Picture Taken by Joni Aveni May 2006 has a cloud figure upper right corner; Second, Third, & Fourth Pictures Taken Daphne Flynn October 2004 have orbs on the building and in the sky and also have figures in the windows.

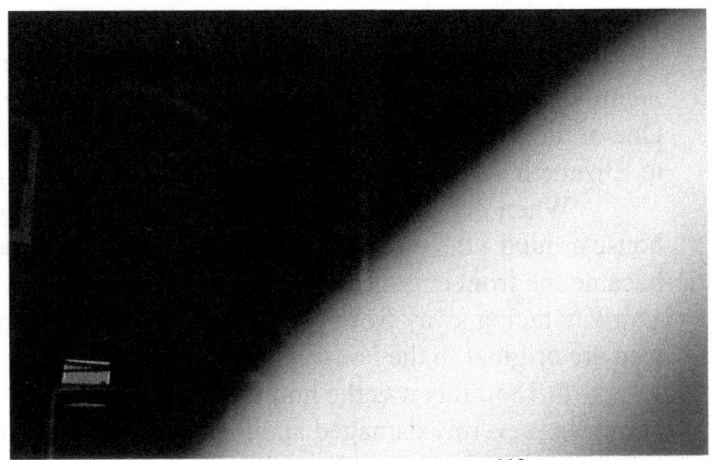

This picture shows a mysterious cloud. [119]

Caroline Street, is named for Caroline, the wife of George the Second, she was a blonde who was considered by some to be attractive. Caroline was a powerful woman for her time. She knew how to control the throne. Does this remind you of *anyone* you know today? You see history *does* repeat itself.

623 Caroline Street[120]

---

[119] Picture Taken by Daphne Flynn October 2004
[120] Picture Taken by Beverly Amberg September 1998 shows a figure in the window

The house known as the Chimneys was built in 1769 facing the sea - because the owner had shipping interests. One of the first owners was a Mr. Glassel who was married to Elizabeth Taylor (a niece of President Zachary Taylor).

When the wing was added on the back it turned the house around - the old back entrance on Caroline Street became the front entrance. This reorientation now has the stairway facing away from you. The floorboards and parlor trim are original to the house.

In 1850 this was the home of Brody Herndon. His home was severely damaged and then occupied by strangers, following the Union Invasion of the town.

His niece, Ellen Herndon, (a resident of New York), married an attorney named Chester Arthur in New York City in 1859. While the Herndon Family of Fredericksburg was known for their allegiance to the Southern cause; the Arthur Family of New York is known for its allegiance to the Northern cause. The only recorded visit of Chester Arthur to Fredericksburg, was recorded after 1862 when he was seen on the streets of town while serving as the Union Quartermaster from New York.

Ellen Herndon Arthur never served as First Lady for she died before Chester Arthur was elected President of the United States.[121]

There are four ghost stories attached to this building:

When the mother went to tuck her son into bed she found two little boys sleeping there.

"Oh he has invited someone over for the evening and did not tell me. I will tuck them both into bed and tomorrow morning I will find out who he is."

She tucked both boys safely into bed and the next morning when her son came down the stairs she asked: "Who did you have over last night?"

---

[121] 'The Romance Stories of The Past' by Helen R. Marler

"I did not have anyone over last night. I was alone."
In a room on the top floor the servers have heard footsteps and seen the shape of a woman. When it was a French restaurant diners would mention seeing a lady on the stairway.

According to legend – During the Union Invasion there was a solider who believed, if you were wounded and you kept walking you would not die. He was wounded and he started walking in this room and he died. Some members of the restaurant staff actually saw a man in a cape pass them in the room.

In the annex on the first floor, there is a little girl, she is weeping and no one knows why she is crying.

During a family gathering in the garden; one of the daughters was playing the piano in the parlor. She paid no attention when the door opened and someone came in and sat down on the bench beside her. She finished playing the piece and turned to see who had joined her – there was no one there.

A picture of the Chimneys with cloudy figures and a few orbs[122]

---

[122] Picture Taken by Daphne Flynn October 2004

This picture shows a distinct orb on the roof.[123]

A picture of a figure in the window to the right of the chimney.[124]

---

[123]Picture Taken by Daphne Flynn October 2004
[124]Picture Taken by Daphne Flynn October 2004

701, 703 & 705 Caroline Street[125]

A picture of 701 Caroline Street with a distinct orb on the right, a cloudy figure across the front, and a figure in the window.[126]

---

[125] Picture is one of series of photographs of Fredericksburg taken in 1927 by Francis Benjamin Johnston. The entire series is available on the internet through the Library of Congress website.
[126] Picture Taken by Teresa and Sara Auth, October 2004

703 Caroline Street[127]

When 703 Caroline Street was a store named Bears Everywhere the owner of the shop would come in to find that overnight the displays were rearranged. Unlocked doors would become locked. There would be times when bears would mysteriously float down from the shelves to the floor.

On one occasion an employee was alone in the building and the presence of someone walked across the room.

This picture of a window display in Bears Everywhere captured a few orbs. Many people see a face in the center pane and the pane to the right center.[128]

---

[127] Picture Taken by Author
[128] Picture Taken by Beverly Amberg September 1998

705 Caroline Street[129]

    Between 1830 and 1850, 705 Caroline Street was the office of William Churchill Beale, a prominent miller and merchant of the town.[130]

    The 700 block of Caroline Street contains buildings form three different centuries. The 18th century mansion on the corner, known as the Chimneys, the 19th century reconstruction of merchants shops and homes extending from the corner of the street and conclude with the 20th century buildings on the corner of Hanover and Caroline Streets.

701 & 711-713 Caroline Street[131]

---

[129] Picture Taken by Author
[130] The True Love Stories of the Past

There are two buildings in this block which are believed to date from the 18th century and to be designed by the same architect. 701 and 711-713 Caroline Street are said to have survived the early fires and the invasions during the War Between the States.

For several years, I repeated the legend, both buildings were designed by a Signer of the Declaration of Independence. The legend was further detailed stating he was the same man who had been the architect of the Octagon House in Washington, D.C.

At this time, I must apologize and correct my error, further historical research has proven this information to be incorrect.

The architect's name was said to be either Lomax or Tayloe. The surnames Lomax and Tayloe do not appear on The Declaration of Independence.

The American Architectural Foundation (AAF) is the third owner of The Octagon House in Washington, D.C. and they have published an extensive history of the house[132].

---

[131] Pictures Taken by Author

[132] The Octagon House remained in the possession of the Tayloe Family until 1902 when the house was purchased and preserved by the American Association of Architects. In 1968 the house was sold to the American Architectural Foundation who has opened it to the public. The picture of the house from the website; maybe a picture taken by Howard Marler: http://www.archfoundation.org/octagon/about/history.htm

The Octagon House was designed by the man who served as the first architect of the United States Capital – William Thornton - *for* John Tayloe III (1770-1828). The Octagon House was built from 1799-1801 and was a winter home until 1817 when it became his full time residence. When the President's Home (now known as the White House) was burned in 1814, Mr. Tayloe's house served as the home of President James Madison and his wife Dolley.

John Tayloe III was the son of John Tayloe II (1721-1779), both father and son lived in a house named Mt. Airy on the Rappahannock River in Richmond County, Virginia. This house still remains in the Tayloe Family.

The Virginia Biographical Encyclopedia describes John Tayloe II (1721-1779) as a Justice of Richmond County and a wealthy planter who may have been one of the most financially endowed and influential people of the time. He completed his home "Mt Airy" on the Rappahannock River in Richmond County, Virginia in 1758. He also had a winter townhouse in Williamsburg, Virginia.

The author further explains that though John Tayloe II had been a friend of George Washington and supporter of liberty - he may not have supported the revolution. When the convention of 1776 elected him to be a member of the first republican council of the state – Mr. Tayloe declined the position.[133]

According to early Virginia land records John Tayloe II owned many acres of land in King George and Spotsylvania Counties and several lots in the City of Fredericksburg. He was the mortgage holder for a Benjamin Johnston for property in Fredericksburg, Virginia in 1774.

While Mr. Tayloe is described as a planter and a Justice; I cannot find whether or not he was an architect. Therefore, if the lots now comprising 701 and 711 Caroline

---

[133] The Virginia Biographical Encyclopedia

Street were owned by Mr. Tayloe, he may or may not, have designed the buildings currently standing on them. Nevertheless, he did *not* design the Octagon House and he was *not* a signer of the Declaration of Independence.

711-713 Caroline Street[134]

      Some research indicates that 711-713 Caroline Street known Richard Johnston Inn may date to 1754 with the floorboards being original to the building. Instead of building above and below, as the other merchants in town, Mr. Johnston had his store on one side and his residence on the other.

      The front of the building contains what may or may not be bullet and ricochet strikes from the invasion of the town in 1862. For many years after the close of the War Between the States we called these strikes our sacred wounds and we did not repair them. Time has passed and things have changed so these sacred wounds are not as numerous as they have been in the past.

---

[134] Picture Taken by Author

This photograph of the front of the building shows the possible bullet strikes and may contain some shadowy figures [135]

The Battle of Fredericksburg is a unique battle in three ways: it takes place in the winter, the throwing of pontoons under heavy artillery fire; and there is intense street fighting in the town. If these are indeed original bullet strikes these marks are a silent witness to that fighting.

The men of the Union Army are invading the town from across the Rappahannock River. They will cross the river in pontoon boats and then, for protection, they will enter through the back of a building and come out the front on the next street.

While the Union Forces are moving forward, the Confederates Forces are moving backward toward the Marye's Heights through the buildings.

Do you see why the buildings and the streets could be haunted?

---

[135] Picture Taken by Teresa and Sarah Auth October 2005

Picture of orbs and mysterious figures inside the building[136]

719 Caroline Street[137]

719 Caroline Street is one of the 20th century buildings in this block and provides evidence that a building does not have to be old to have haunting stories. The shop owners have had haunting experiences.

When they first rented the building they would hear sounds and noticed the light switches kept being turned off

---

[136] Picture Taken by Beverly Amberg September 1998
[137] Picture Taken by Anonymous Donor

and on. Little children and dogs did not want to go up the stairs to the second floor.

A customer, who believes in ghosts, told them they had a ghost of an elderly man who had died on the premises and he is very glad for their company in the building. She said his name was Vincent or Victor.

Now when they hear bumping and noises they will say "I hear you" and the noise stops.

On occasion someone will call the husband or wife by name and they realize that is Vincent.

Vincent seems to be an electrician. There was a halogen lamp on the second floor which was not working properly. One evening just before closing the lamp was being most difficult. Since it was late and they were ready to go home they unplugged the lamp and removed the bulb.

The next morning when they came in and went upstairs they found the bulb was in the lamp and it was plugged in – the lamp worked perfectly.

A picture taken in the front window showing mysterious figures and perhaps a face, above the Cigar Store Indian.[138]

---

[138] Picture Taken by Daphne Flynn October 2004

This picture or the second floor window shows curtains – this window does not have curtains. Some people see a shape in the right side of the window.[139]

Due to the traumas of the 18th and 19th centuries you cannot eat anywhere in this town without a chance of a haunting experience.

717 Caroline Street[140]

A previous owner of the restaurant at 717 Caroline Street told us that the building is haunted. He stated that an ax murder had taken place in the building and when he first rented out the apartments upstairs the tenants would find

---

[139] Picture Taken by Chris Bloomquist June 2004
[140] Picture Taken by Author

themselves pushed down the stairway, but this situation changed over time.

In the restaurant portion of the building the staff would place a plate on the top shelf and the plate would float down.

A server would provide you with a glass of water and somehow the glass would split in half down the middle.

The lady's rest room had a push door with no locks. Nevertheless there would be times when a line would form outside of the door because it was locked from inside. After a few minutes, someone would try the door and it would swing open with no resistance.

816 Caroline Street [141]

Rumor states 816 Caroline Street is called Spirits because it is haunted. If you are in the bar having pizza with your friends, everyone hears someone coming up the stairs, there is noise and confusion. You all turn to see who has arrived and there is no one there.

The boxes in the building are mysteriously rearranged, alarms come on; and lights go off and on. There was once a series of burned out light bulbs – when they went to change them they found that the bulbs had actually been twisted into the sockets until they were broken.

---

[141] Picture Taken by Author

At night when all the customers have left, and the staff is working in the office, they will see figures of people walking across the screen on the security monitors.

The kitchen, located in the basement, is said to be haunted by a Confederate Soldier. The cooks have had incidents in the kitchen where objects, including knives, have been projected across the room.

One evening a member of the staff went down to the kitchen and while he is standing there a loaf of bread passed between him and the chef. The bread landed on the floor by the chef's feet. The chef picked up the loaf and said "I wish he would stop doing that – that is the third loaf he has thrown at me today".

801 Hanover Street[142]

In the 19th century 801 Hanover Street was the home and business of Anthony Buck who was an auctioneer. The knowledge that Mr. Buck would have sold all forms of personal property for individuals at auction including slaves

---

[142] This picture is mistakenly identified as 801 Hanover Street is it a picture of 801 Caroline Street taken from the Hanover Street side. Picture is one of series of photographs of Fredericksburg taken in 1927 by Francis Benjamin Johnston. The entire series is available on the internet through the Library of Congress website.

– provides one with a basis of trauma for what could be possible haunting stories.

The building is now a restaurant and there have been a few accounts of mysterious events.

The most interesting story comes from a prior owner's relative. She stated that when she was a child her uncle would playfully blow on her neck. Recently, when she dined here felt her uncle once more come and blow on her neck.

I have met people who have heard, on this street, the sound of soldiers marching; horses hooves; and the caissons – they have stated that the noise begins about three days before the anniversary of one of the Civil War Battles and continues growing louder until the day of the event.

We have heard, on our phantom walk, the sound of the artillery from across the river and some of us have seen muzzle flashes at night. When I mentioned this to members of the police department, they told me they have received calls from Stafford County asking why we are setting off munitions in town at night.

Hanover Street is named for the House of Hanover in England. When Queen Anne died in 1716 she was the last acceptable Stuart, so the throne was bestowed upon George the 1st Hanover, Germany. George the 1st ruled England from Germany. His son, George the 2nd was the last British ruler to actually ride with his troops into battle. They both refused to learn English and spoke only German on the British throne.

As stated earlier, the town is named for Frederick, the son of George 2nd it is Fredericksburg is because the royal family spoke German.

It was the son of Frederick, George the 3rd for whom we wrote the nursery rhyme "Georgie Porgie Puddin and Pie kissed the girls and made them cry. When the big boys came out to play Georgie Porgie ran away." This refers to Fat

George the man who started the Revolution ~~ political mud slinging has gone on for generations.

In the 19th century, we wanted to teach our children how to ice skate, so we made all of our skates with the wheels in one line.

When we would write our letters we would use an ink well shaped like a snail. The finished letter would be carried through a series of friends or through the US Mail. We called it "snail mail" because it took so long to arrive.

801 Sophia Street[143]

In 1807 this was the site of the Bank of Virginia. In the 19th century we had a more direct method of security in our banks - they were occupied buildings so no one would break in.

In this case, the building was occupied by the head cashier, William Roberts, his wife Isabella, and their new born son John.

On October 7, 1807 a fire began in the home of William Stannard in the 1200 block of Princess Anne Street. The fire spread through the town; consuming forty four city blocks; leaped across the river and burned part of the

---

[143] Picture Taken by Author

Washington Family Farm (George Washington's Boyhood Home).

By divine providence, there were three men nearby who helped rescue Isabella and the baby - they placed them in the garden. When you read the accounts of the fire of 1807 they state no one died - but Isabella had died within the month. Could it be they had not heard of smoke inhalation? Isabella was buried in the Masonic Cemetery. We have of a lady in a cape in the Masonic Cemetery could she be Isabella?.[144]

In the 1820s the Shiloh Baptist Church was erected here. In 1855 the 200 white members sold the church to the 600 free and slave black members who named their church The African Baptist Church. The African Baptist Church became a surgery.

After the War Between the States the name was changed back to Shiloh (meaning peace) Baptist Church.

In 1886 the building, weakened by damage from the war and by flooding, collapsed and the congregation split into two parts and fought for four years over where to rebuild.

In 1890 they resolved the issue by building two new churches Shiloh Old Site Baptist Church on this lot and Shiloh New Site Baptist Church on Princess Anne Street.

Some people believe the church is haunted. They have heard the church bells chime, sometimes at night, when the church is empty.

The area behind the building is of more interest as a possibly haunted spot. May people have noticed a cold spot behind the church.

Ladies will complain that cold fingers touch their faces as they walk through the cold spot. This is where additional footsteps will follow us, sometimes as many as three sets of the distinctive heel plates of the brogans will

---

[144] This picture is shown in the Masonic Cemetery Section of this work

join us. Men in gray uniforms will feel an animosity surrounding them; while men dressed in blue uniforms will feel an acceptance. On one of our walks some men dressed as soldiers stepped off the pavement onto the grass and the mysterious footsteps followed them.

The sound is believed to be the metallic heel plates of three Union Soldiers who died in the African Baptist Church

One evening as we proceeded away from the church, toward the home of the silversmith house; a lady in 19th century clothing who was walking with us suddenly stopped because something was holding the edge of her skirt. There was nothing in on the ground or no one near her to detain her in that fashion.

The Front of Shiloh Old Site with several orbs[145]

Orbs and cloudy figures appear behind the church.[146]

---

[145] Picture Taken by Michael W Brown October 2006
[146] Picture Taken by Daphne Flynn October 2004

A picture of a mysterious figure and glow.[147]

The Rappahannock River[148]

The Rappahannock River is named for the Rappahannock Indian Tribe. They are part of Powhatan's Confederacy. Powhatan is a mighty chieftain who has eighty body guards and several thousand men in his confederacy.

In 1608 John Smith explored this river, and from him we learn it is over twenty feet deep and very clear. There are enormous fish, panthers, bears, and there are Indians.

There is an altercation with the Indians and they make peace; which is the beginning of the end of the Indian's reign in the region.

---

[147] Picture Taken by Beverly Amberg September 1998
[148] Picture from a postcard a postcard postmarked November 12, 1908. Copyright: The Rotograph Co., N.Y. City. (Germany)

Pocahontas, Powhatan's daughter, was kidnapped from this river and taken to Jamestown where they wanted to force her father into treaty agreements.

While in Jamestown, she was baptized a Christian and changed her name to Rebecca. Here she met John Rolfe and married him.

The governor of Virginia sent the Rolfe's to England on a fund raising expedition. While in England she contracted small pox – she died on the dock trying to board a ship to return home to Virginia.

When the town is announced in 1728, the Indian village of Seacobeck is dwindling in size, due to the white man's diseases.

The Indians are concerned because the white man has taken their land, their population and now they are going to take the river.

The mighty Shaman of the tribe will go to an island on the river, raise his hands to heaven, and pronounce a curse. As long as this town stands, the river will be cursed.

Fredericksburg became the tenth largest seaport in the world and serviced over thirty ships each day coming from one hundred and twenty ports world wide.

In the 18th century entire ships would disappear - they would vanish – cargo, vessel and all.

In the 19th century the reason the Union Army wanted this town was due to its location. The town had the train system from Aquia to Richmond; the main thoroughfare to the west traveled through the tow; and there was the river. Could all the confusion, all the contention, and all the bloodshed be part of the curse on the river?

In the 20th century, people are advised not wade in the river and they further warned not to swim in the river the swift undercurrent takes people away and the bodies are not recovered for several weeks.

When there is a drowning on the river, people who have grown up here for generations, will look at one another and say "The curse on the river."

This picture shows small lights and orbs by the river [149]

813 Sophia Street[150]

    The building which serves as the Center For Creative Arts, was built in 1796 by James White, a silver smith in the town. The interior walls are original to 1796 and in the basement you can still view the original hand hewn beams in the ceiling.
    The foundation is formed from the Rappahannock Sand Stone quarried here in the river. Sandstone is a soft porous rock; birds build their nests in the sandstone quarries. It is the sandstone which has saved this building from the flooding of the river because the water comes in and it flows back out.

---
[149] Picture Taken by Daphne Flynn October 2004
[150] Picture Taken by Author

The building has survived fires, floods, and the War Between the States. If you study the sandstone foundation on the back of the building below the noggin (the section where the wooden siding covers the brick of the house) you will see about 13 cannon strikes from where the Union Army shelled the town from across the river.

The cannon strikes in this picture can be seen on far left side; to the left and right side of the chimney; there are many grape shot wounds on the chimney; on the upper right corner there are two strikes. [151]

On the third floor to the left and right of the chimney you will see two windows. In the window on the left people see a figure in white stepping forward and retreating backward. More recently people have seen a figure appearing in the window on the right of the chimney.

If you have a camera, you will want to study the window through your camera because we have had people see things through their cameras that other people cannot see.

---

[151] Pictures Taken by Author

These pictures show figures in the windows, and orbs and clouds around the building.[152]

---

[152] Pictures 1, 2, and 3 were Taken By Teresa and Sara Auth October 2004 Picture 4 was Taken by Teresa and Sara Auth October 2005

A series of four pictures showing mysterious figures coming and going.[153]

---

[153] Pictures taken by Denise Bryant August 2003

More pictures of cloud figures and images in the windows[154]

---

[154] Pictures 1, 2, & 3 were Taken by Daphne Flynn October 2004;
Picture 4 was Taken by Anonymous Donor October 2000

Many people see a man in the air between the dormer and the chimney.[155]

As you view the side of the building you will notice a door that appears out of place, until you put yourself back in the 18th century. There was a pulley above the door and when it was necessary to have items delivered or shipped out a wagon would be drawn underneath the door and the barrels or bales would be raised and lowered into the bed of the wagon.

Take a few moments to look under the steps and study the beautiful stone archway at the front of the building. You will find the Rappahannock Sandstone being used as steps, foundations and windowsills throughout the town.[156]

---

[155] Picture Taken by Beverly Amberg September 1998
[156] Picture Taken by Tom and Brenda Nay

The Wells House[157]

They call it the Wells House because Captain Wells of New York subleased it as a boarding house before the War Between the States. A few years ago it was known as Romantic Beginnings - A Bridal and Formal Wear Shop.

The staff of the shop would hear guitar music and they would experience items falling repeatedly from the shelves. One day there was a strange sound upstairs and they found a picture had fallen; whereas they were busy with customers, they turned the frame around and placed the picture against the wall. Upon hearing another strange sound from upstairs they returned to find the frame had been turned so the picture was facing out.

They would find bridal gowns were rearranged; and sometimes the gowns would disappear and later return.

One day a gown had disappeared and they could find it nowhere in the building; this caused great concern for it was to be picked up by the bride the next day. The date of delivery arrived and the bride failed to come for her gown. A few days later the bridal gown re-appeared along with the

---

[157] Picture Taken by Michael Matthieu August 1998. The house was empty at the time of the picture. There were no curtains in the window and no people inside – many people see curtains on the window and people inside of the house.

news that the bride had not come to pick it up because she had died.

Many times customers would be standing by the door preparing to leave and a member of the staff would have to reach past them to open the previously unlocked door.

The haunting stories may be linked to the so-called love story associated with this house. Captain Wells, was a steam ship captain from New York who was accused of being a Confederate Spy. There is no proof that he was a spy nevertheless he did take in a boarder who was a Union Spy - Ortson Kirby of Pennsylvania.

Mr. Kirby who wrote a book, and from him we learn that the Captain had twelve children; one of whom was fifteen year old Geno who played the song *Juanita* on her guitar for him while he sat down on the couch (It was Ortson Kirby who warned Captain Wells that the Union Army thought he might be a spy.)

The Union Army did not like this, and according to his own account, they came to the Wells House and took him out of the front door. Geno is following them; she has a handkerchief.

Ortson Kirby took the handkerchief; kissed her, and said: "I will never forget you. I will come back and marry you."

Some versions of the story recount that he was across the Rappahannock during the invasion and that he was concerned about the Wells Family who were in the basement of the house.

Ortson Kirby's later actions do not show that was as devoted to Geno as he had said. While Geno died waiting for his return: he had gotten married and had a family of three children.

You might find of interest that Captain Wells was concerned that one of the Armies might take his steamship so he hid the vessel in a cove on the river. The ship was found and was confiscated. Sometime later his family was starving and while he was rowing his boat down river to find something for them to eat he was arrested for attempted blockade running by the Union Army.

The story continues with two of his daughters seeking assistance from President Lincoln in his behalf. Captain Wells did survive the ordeal and would later return to New York and open a hotel. Ortson Kirby came to see him!

When we stand in front of the Wells House, a man in 19th century clothing has been seen in the window to the left of the door.

When this building was Romantic Beginnings the owners painted the house a light yellow with black shutters The shutter to the left of the door was crooked, they replaced that shutter; and then another shutter would become crooked. We noticed when the house was last repainted and new shutters were put in place these shutters started losing their slats. This house does not like shutters.

Orbs appear on the front of the house.[158]

---

[158] Picture Taken by Denise Bryant June 2003

Pictures showing lights and figures in the house.[159]

When we view the house from the corner of George and Sophia streets we will see a white figure in the second floor window on the right. When Romantic Beginnings was moving out we saw a figure in the window and thought that they had left something white in the room and would be back to retrieve it.

Virginia Currents, A local PBS program, was coming to film our Phantom Walk and on the day of the filming there were people in the house. So I stopped in and requested that if I helped move the items, could we make sure that nothing was left in the windows for I did not want to have objects mistaken for ghosts. We went up to the second floor – the room was barren, even the rug was gone.

"What is the white object we see in the window at night" I asked

"I don't know what you're talking about" was the reply.

The new owners told me that they were not there at night and there was no electricity in the building. That night and other nights we would approach the building and see a single light on in one of the rooms or the basement. From George Street side we would see a figure in white walking across the window on the left and there was this single figure in white in the window on the right.

I thought it might be a dirty window pane so waited for the owners to settle in. They moved in, painted the

---

[159] Pictures Taken by Daphne Flynn October 2004

exterior, thoroughly cleaned the window panes and the figure is still there.

When the house was on the market again, I contacted the realtor and requested that she open the blinds on the second floor. She not only opened the blinds but came on one of walks. When we turned to look in the windows she said "What is that?"

"I hoped that you could tell us what it was"

She replied that there was nothing in the room and we learned that night that while the house is fully heated and air conditioned the services were not on at the time; so the white figure was not related to the heating or air conditioning system.

Four pictures of the mysterious figure in the window on the first and second floor.[160]

Three pictures of the end of the building showing the mysterious figure in the window – two of these pictures show that the shutters are missing.[161]

---

[160] Pictures Taken by Anonymous Donors
[161] The top Picture Taken by Daphne Flynn October 2004. The picture to the left Taken by Beverly Amberg September 1998 The picture to the right Taken by Joni Aveni May 2006.

Corner of William and Sophia Streets[162]

    They call it the old stone warehouse, the foundation was built about 1754 with these sandstone walls being added about 1812. This was not a tobacco warehouse, it is composed of the wrong material, a tobacco warehouse was a wooden two story structure; this building served as a dry goods warehouse.

---

[162] The top picture is from Oscar H. Darter 1957 Colonial Fredericksburg and Neighborhood In Perspective. P.160. New York: Twayne Publishers. The bottom Picture Taken by Author

This is actually a four story building; the bottom two stories were covered when the bridge was raised due to flooding. The original four stories can still be viewed from the river side of the building.

If you compare the picture from before 1957 with the more recent image, you will see additional rows of doors and windows in this building, and also a dormer on the roof.

In 1913 we cured salt fish by a secret formula, which preserved the wood work inside the building. During the War Between the States this will serve a temporary morgue. Can you imagine four stories of bodies?

As we approach the building from the lower Sophia Street side many people see a figure between the two windows. People say it resembles a Mayan figure or a man with a moustache and glasses. [163]

Between the door and the window to its right you will see the shape of a hat, a face, and shoulders - he is looking right at you. The Mayan figure, or man with glasses, will fade out the hat, face and shoulders will not – this image will turn his head and follow you as your travel up the street.

This picture has three images of interest. First, between the door and the window there is the image of a hat,

---

[163] Picture Taken by Author

a face, and shoulders. Second, on the electrical box in front of the building, is a figure in a cape. Third, in the lower window to the right, you can see a face on the left hand side.[164]

 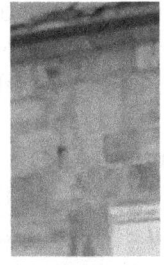 

These smaller isolated images show the figure of a hat, face, and shoulders (above left). The picture above to the right shows a face in the window.[165]

The picture to the immediate right shows the Mayan head next to the window.

When we observe the building from the front people may see a large white head or figure on the roof extending

---

[164] Picture Taken by Jeannine Thornton September 1997
[165] First and Third Pictures Taken by Jeannine Thornton - Second and Fourth Pictures Taken by Author.

from the peak downward; they describe it as looking an Indian or a large white skull.

Many people have seen a black cat by the door, fading in and out, as they watch him

To the right of the door is the shape of a hat, a face, and shoulders. I called it the rock deformation; but people will say he is waving, he is turning, he has a beard, or even say he is wearing a jacket.

If you follow the rain gutter to the downspout; you will see where the downspout curves in - to the left of the curve there is a distinct profile of someone facing the bridge. You will see the eyebrow, one eye, the nose, the chin, and a brown collar.

Immediately on the opposite side to the downspout you will see another profile facing the building to the right. They are back to back.

We have had people tell us there are figures in 18th century clothing walking in front of the building. We have others tell us writing appears on the walls.

This picture shows the image behind the trash can and three images between the window and the building to the right. [166]

---

[166] Picture Taken by Daphne Flynn October 2004

This enlargement of the above photo by the down spout; contains four images. There are two beside the window, and two back to back against the downspout.

This picture has a white figure on the roof and also shows the hat, face and shoulders by the door plus a profile by the down spout.[167]

---

[167] Picture Taken by Jeanine Thornton September 1997

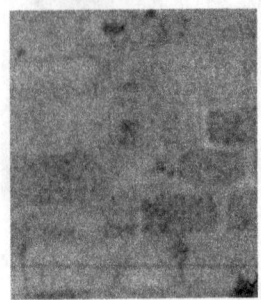
This enlargement of the above picture shows a different image to the left of the door.

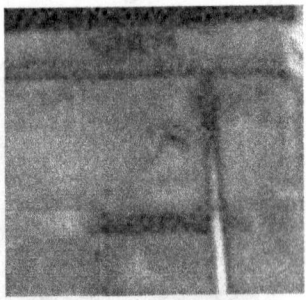
The enlarged section of the image by the down spout shows a distinct profile.

Pictures showing orbs on the front of The Old Stone Warehouse; in addition there are images by the door and down spout. [168]

---

[168] Top Picture Taken by Anonymous Donor
Bottom Picture Taken by Kelly Doyle May 2002

If you look at the end of the old stone warehouse where the triangle is formed by the roof above the window you may see an Indian in full head dress. Some people describe him as the Indian on the buffalo nickel.

To the left of the window you will see a long white line - that is an officer's sash, which extends around the waist of a soldier. Above this line you will see a breast plate. Directly above the breast plate you will see a head. If you can make him out you will see over his right shoulder is a rifle and below the waist band there is only one leg[169].

Directly below the window you might see the head of a horse running toward the bridge. In the bottom corner of the building you can see both a cauldron and a cannon.

Sometimes when we are standing here at night people can see a figure forming on the roof

---

[169] Picture Taken by Marcus Lawrence

Picture taken inside of the Old Stone Warehouse with a mysterious figure appearing on the film – the husband and wife are taking pictures of each other the mysterious figure showed up on this picture but not in the video.[170]

Has anyone ever taken the time to tell what the star is for on a building? Sometimes it will be a star, a diamond or an S.

This is an 18th century feature which is actually an iron bar holding the building together so it will not bow out. This method of construction seems to have ended about 1834; but has been revived and is now used in Charleston, South Carolina as a means of holding buildings together in case of earth quake.

On our Phantom Walks we would often have shoelaces, strings, hair bows, wrap around skirts and even underpinning become untied. Buckles were not immune for we would have the buckles on gators and belts become opened.

We have also had the opposite experience where strings have become tied into knots. There was one evening when we had a group join us for a phantom bus trip - when I boarded the bus my underpinnings came undone. The next

---

[170] Picture Taken by Scott Minot

day they joined us for a pure history experience. When they came off of the bus one passenger said:

"I need to tell that last night I wore a sweat shirt with strings hanging down the front. I took this sweat shirt and hung it up in the bathroom my hotel room. When I got up this morning the strings were tied in knots. "

Another evening a mother and son joined us for a walk; as they traveled through town the mother was on the right and the son was to her left. They took pictures and enjoyed the journey but experienced no haunting events until they stopped for food afterwards. When the mother was seated she looked down at her shoe and some one had tied a knot in the string on the left side of her left shoe.

She then examined her son's shoe and discovered a matching knot on the end of the lace on the right side of his right shoe. It was as if someone had stood between them and tied their shoe strings in artistic knots.

A picture of the mother and son shoe laces tied by someone who had stood between them[171]

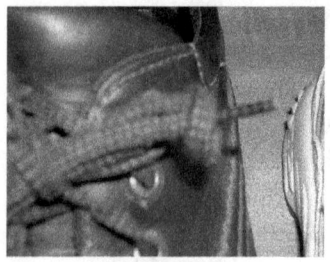 

Sophia was the name of the wife, the mother, and a sister of George 2nd. Sophia Street is believed to have been named in honor of his sister, who became the mother of Frederick the Great – King of Prussia.

Sophia Street was the site of wharves and warehouses. The main crop was tobacco placed in large

---

[171] Picture Taken by Anonymous Donor

barrels called hogs heads and rolled into the two story wooden warehouse. You were paid in a tobacco warehouse receipt which would be used instead of money with the merchants of the town. Don't you still use substitute items for money with your merchants?

In the 18th century our politicians and clergy were paid in tobacco. In the Commonwealth of Virginia our politicians still have a great interest in the tobacco trade – an interest which has lasted for over three hundred years.

Chatham Manor or the Lacy House [172]

On the Stafford side of the Rappahannock River stands a house built in the 1770s by William Fitzhugh, a great supporter of the revolution. He named his house Chatham Manor after the Earl of Chatham - William Pitt for whom Pittsburg, Pennsylvania and Pittsfield, Massachusetts are named. William Pitt was the colonist's friend in Parliament.

After the Revolution all of Mr. Fitzhugh's friends and relatives kept coming to see him. They ate him out of house and home; he sold his house and moved to Alexandria, Virginia to escape them.

---

[172] Picture from a vintage comercialchrome postcard Published by RA Kispaugh, Fredericksburg, VA.

During the War Between the States, this is the home of J Horace Lacy, who was arrested by the Federal Forces in 1862 and sent to the Federal Prison in Washington, D.C. His house served as the headquarters for seventy-two year old General Edwin V. "Bull" Sumner, USA; with General Ambrose Burnside's headquarters being located farther north.

From this house, the Union Army directed the invasion of the town, and to this house the wounded and dying returned. If a soldier survived the surgery, he was sent by boat or wagon to Washington, D.C. Do you see why so many men died?

The wing on the left end served as the surgery. In this room were Walt Whitman, Clara Barton, and a female civilian surgeon, Mary Walker. The method of surgery was amputation with the tables being placed by the windows. The surgeon threw the arms and legs out of the windows. There are so many limbs the pile will come up to the window sills. These limbs are buried by wagon loads on the property and people today complain of a strange odor from the grounds.

The Lacy House in March of 1863[173]

---

[173] This picture was taken by Timothy H O'Sullivan (1840-1882) It is part of a Library of Congress Collection that is available online.

Many years ago a room in the left wing was used for the re-creation of a surgery. While they were working in this room, the people looked up to see a man in a blue uniform standing in the door way. He stood there with his arms folded watching them and then exited down the hall. When they asked the ranger who this man was - they were told that no one had come in and no one had gone out of the hallway.

One day during one of our *Feel The Fury Serie*s I was escorting two men around the house. They saw a man in 19th century clothing watching them through the window - they searched the house and found no one in 19th century clothing inside.

On another occasion, a man arrived early to take part in a re-enactment. He parked his car in the nearly empty parking lot and carried his first box to the site. As he turned the corner of the house he was surprised to find many Union Soldiers were already in place. He put his box on the ground and returned to his car for the next load. This time when he came around the house, the only thing in site was the box he had left a few minutes before.

In the dawn and in the dusk, people in the buildings on the town side of the river have seen cannons lining the hills with the sentries standing beside them. One individual who witnessed this scene looked through collections of Civil War photographs and found a picture of the Union artillery which matched what he had seen.

The last owner of this house was John Lee Pratt, a Chairman of General Motors; having no heirs, Mr. Pratt willed the house to the National Park Service.

Amelia Street is named for the second eldest daughter of King George. She was engaged to her cousin Frederick – everyone knew they would marry. The engagement was broken by the father of Frederick, who forced him to marry Catherine of Brunswick. Frederick became Frederick The Great, King of Prussia.

Amelia remained single when she died at the age of seventy years it was discovered that she had always carried Frederick's picture next to her heart.[174]

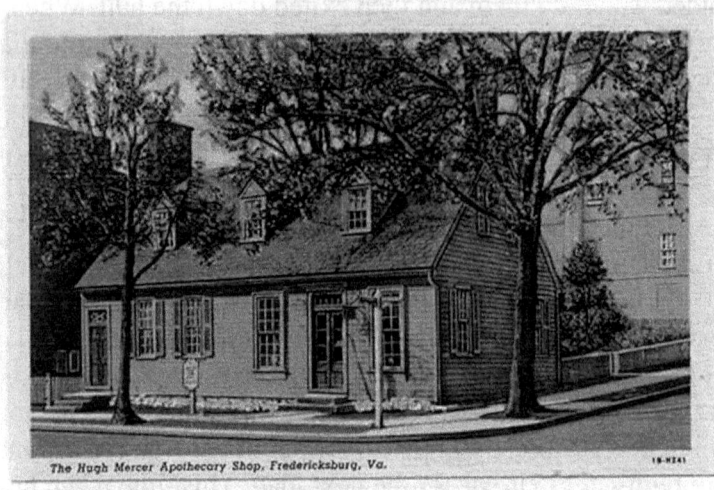

1020 Caroline Street[175]

Hugh Mercer was a political refugee from Scotland who arrived on this continent during the French and Indian War. Dr. Mercer knows how it feels when he sets your arm because he set his own arm.

In 1761 he came to Fredericksburg and opened an apothecary and a surgery. Dr Mercer became a well-liked man in town. In 1776 he stated "I will defend my adopted country. No matter what, I will do what the Lord asks me to do"

In January, 1777 he was serving in the Battle of Princeton in New Jersey. The British believed he was George Washington so they shot the horse out from under him. When he fell, twelve redcoats swiftly surrounded him

---

[174] "The Romance Stories of the Past" by Helen R Marler
[175] This picture is from a Genuine Curteich –Chicago "C.T. Art Colortone Post Card (Reg. U.S. Pat Off.) published by RA Kishpaugh,

and stabbed Hugh Mercer twenty-four times. He lingered nine days until he gave everything he had for our freedom.

Hugh Mercer still affects you today. Thorough his daughter he became the ancestor of the seven Patton Brothers of Culpeper County, Virginia; who served in the Confederacy. Through them he became the ancestor of General George Patton of Second World War Fame.

Thorough his sons he became the ancestor of General Hugh Weedon Mercer of Savannah, Georgia who was the great-grandfather of Johnny Mercer (1909-1976) the composer.

The 18th century building, where the APVA honors Hugh Mercer, was first owned by Henry Mitchell who used it as his home and shop. Henry Mitchell was an outspoken supporter of the King and was opposed to the revolution. His attitude would lead to his being driven out of town and therefore, he was in his native Scotland during the Revolution.

In 1820 this building was the home of David and Mildred Henderson and became known as Henderson's Corner. Here he had a shop on the first floor with a winter's kitchen on the hill in the back. I am not sure where he kept the eleven children. I think the Henderson children help to haunt this building.

The current staff will be in the back office and somehow the door is opened without their hearing anyone enter. When they check on the noise and confusion they find no one there.

Many people who visit the Apothecary will find their shoe laces tied together. The ladies who work here have learned that they must tie their aprons and skirts in a certain way or the ties become undone.

Even when the layers are tied correctly you might find that your apron string is caught on a crevice in the counter. It is something a child might do.

You need to be aware Hugh Mercer is believed to be one of the people who helped drive Mr. Mitchell out of town before the Revolution. Now they honor Hugh Mercer in Henry Mitchell's building.

Everyday the admission fees balance to the penny. At the end of the month the books are off by one to three dollars. Sometimes members of the staff will hear the sound of breaking glass; or see a man in 18th century clothing walking through the door.

The most telling story about the return of Mr. Mitchell is the young lady who reported to work with a school paper accounting the virtues of the American Government tucked in the bottom of her book bag.

She placed the bag in the office, changed her clothing and reported for work. When her shift ended she found that someone had reached down inside the bag and had torn up that particular paper.

As you approach the building from across Amelia Street you may see a figure in the right dormer. If the figure does appear it disappears as you cross the street.

Photographs of the window at night reveal a curtain. There is no curtain in the window.

A picture of the right dormer showing a curtain[176]

---

[176] Picture Taken by Beverly Amberg September 1998

Pictures of the front of the building showing a possible image in the window and orbs and figures[177]

---

[177] Picture top leftTaken by Daphne Flynn October 2004; Picture top right Taken by Beverly Amberg September 1998; Picture bottom left Taken by Anonymous Donor; Picture bottom right Taken by Marcus Lawrence.

In October of 1995, Connie Peters took three pictures in a row of the Apothecary Shop. The middle picture contained these two definite shapes. There is a figure in the window and a second figure outside of the window. [178]

If you study the dormers on the front of the building at night you will see there is no light coming from with in. The street lights are located in three places one in the tree to the left of the building; one across the street in the trees below the level of the dormers and the ones in the intersection.

The back of the building is where cameras fail; or refuse to work - batteries have been known to fall out. If your camera works you may capture the picture of a ghost. Stand so you can see in the dormer on the Amelia Street end of the building. You may or may not see a glow coming from the window –sometimes it is a golden glow, or white, or maybe even red.

---

[178] Picture Taken by Connie Peters RN October 1995

If the flash on the camera works when you try to take a picture of this dormer you may see a curtain or a figure appear. There is no curtain the window.

The lady who oversees the apothecary tells us that years ago the lights were on separate switches. Sometimes she would be told by the neighbors that had been lights on at night and people walking around.

She thought that was due to light switches being accidentally left on. Now all the power is on one switch and we see lights on at night. The upstairs has no lighting or connections and we see lights upstairs at night.

With this in mind, people have seen a candle flame in the right dormer, a blue light in the center dormer, and a bright flame or glow in the left dormer.

On several occasions we have seen a glow in the right dormer that looked as if someone had removed a lampshade leaving the lighted bare bulb exposed.

These two pictures of the left dormer show a curtain or a figure.[179]

---

[179] Picture on left Taken by Beverly Amberg September 1998
Picture on right Taken by Anonymous Donor

The picture on the left shows a possible figure in dormer while the one on the right has a figure forming. [180]

The picture on the left shows white cloudy figures while the one on the right captured some orbs [181]

Another picture of a possible figure in the left dormer[182]

---

[180] Pictures Taken by Daphne Flynn October 2004
[181] Pictures Taken by Missy Morgan September 2002
[182] Picture Taken by Kelly Tyson 2003

Two more pictures of figure in left dormer. [183]

A picture showing a mysterious candlelight in the right dormer.[184]

A picture of mysterious lights in the building[185]

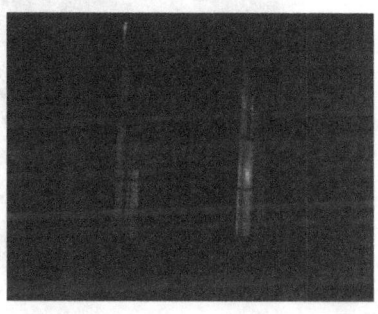

---

[183] Picture on left Taken by Ryan Griffiths June 1997
Picture on right Taken by Joani Aveni May 2006
[184] Picture Taken by Beverly Amberg September 1998
[185] Picture Taken by Marcus Lawrence

Two pictures showing orbs on the roof and in the back of the building[186]

---
[186] Pictures Taken by Nick Ierardi November 2001

In this picture there is a small white dot on the back of the building and there are orbs elsewhere

In this picture the small white dot has expanded in size.

The expanded figure has moved to the right of the building.

The figure has moved farther to the right of the building.

In the last picture of the series the figure is now a dot in the herb garden and there is an orb on the roof. [187]

Corner of Princess Anne and Amelia Street[188]

---

[187] The series of five Pictures were Taken by Traci Ball
[188] Picture from a penny post card Published by Louis Kaufmann & Sons. Baltimore, MD. Made in the U. S. A. (Publishers of Local Views)

The Fredericksburg Baptist Church was established in 1804. This edifice was erected in 1855 when the two-hundred white members sold the building on Sophia Street to the six-hundred black members, free and slave who named their building the African Baptist.

The minister during the construction, and after, was William Broaddus. an educator, who was also the trustee of Columbian College (now known George Washington University). There is a town legend stating the architect may have been James Renwick who also designed St Patrick's Cathedral in New York.

The church became a surgery; the baptismal font a bath tub; and the pews beds for the wounded soldiers. The building was severely damaged services were not held here from December 1862 until April 1865.

The returning members found holes in the roof and walls; the windows were shattered; and the pews and furniture were ripped out and destroyed. They determined that they would restore and improve what they had lost. The present Fredericksburg Baptist Church stands as a tribute to their faith and commitment to the Lord.

There are still bullet and cannon marks in the spire and in the 1960s a live shell was discovered embedded in the walls.

People see lights come on in the building at night and they see faces in the windows.

This picture is of a figure down the side of the church spire. Some people believe they see a solider in a Zouave Uniform holding a flag.[189]

The Zouave Uniform was used by volunteer units from both sides of the war and was based on a then famous Zouave Battalion of the French Army. The French had adopted this flamboyant design from their Algerian opponents in the 1830s.

These uniforms consisted of bright red balloon pants, a blue vest, a blue jacket and, a red fez (some even wore turbans).The attractive trim and colors became a fashionable item for women's clothing while it made the soldier wearing it a much easier target for the enemy.[190]

---

[189] Picture Taken by Anonymous Donor
[190] Picture From the Smithsonian Institution Web Site
http://www.civilwar.si.edu/soldiering_zuoave.html

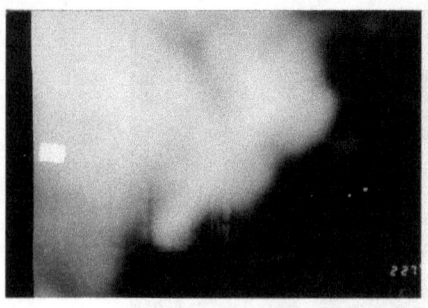 

These pictures of the corner of Princess Anne and Amelia Street show clouds and orbs around the Baptist Church.[191]

Princess Anne Street is named for a daughter of George 2nd who was known as an artist, a linguist, and a musician. She was born in Germany, and married William of Orange and upon his death became the ruler of Holland.

Corner of Amelia and Princess Anne Street[192]

---

[191] Picture on the left Taken by Teresa and Sara Auth, October 2005; Picture on the right Taken by Dylan Waugh October 1996
[192] Picture Taken by Author

The house on the corner of Amelia and Princess Anne Streets was the home of Dr. John Hall a town druggist before and during the War Between the States.

His drug store, on the corner of Caroline and William Streets, was raided twice by the Federal Forces during their invasions of the town. [193]

The home property actually consists of three buildings: The Slave Quarters; The Main Home; and a rare 19th century professional office building.

As we discussed earlier, soldiers of the 19th century had a great fear of being buried unknown This fear was addressed by using a form of ident-i-tag placed around the neck. The Confederate Cemetery serves as an example of how valid this fear was – of the over 3400 soldiers buried in the cemetery only 644 are identified.

19th century graffiti is composed of name and/or unit. The wall of the professional office building bears what maybe units from the invasion of the town.

In 1864 there is a battle in Williamsburg, Virginia which was won by General McClellan. The citizens of Fredericksburg heard the news of this battle from a The New York Times brought into the town.

A few days later, a Richmond paper brought into town, will bear the casualty list of the men we had lost in that battle. There was a town in Tennessee where every soldier had died, never returning home. Could soldiers have left their names and units, in case you came looking, you would know where to find them? [194] [195]

---

[193] Picture is from Oscar H. Darter 1957 Colonial Fredericksburg and Neighborhood In Perspective. P. 160.New York: Twayne Publishers.
[194] See also The Corner of Princess Anne and George Street
[195] Pictures Taken by Author

1106 Princess Anne Street [196]

The first owner of this home was John Allen who built the left end in the late 1740s. By 1862 the house has had been extended to its present length and was the home of William Broaddus the Minister of the Baptist Church. General Pope arrested William Broaddus and eighteen other men of the town sending them to Capital Prison in Washington, D.C. Rev. Broaddus rode with Belle Boyd to arrange a prisoner exchange.

During the invasion of the town in 1862, the Union Army came up from the river. The Confederate soldiers were in the houses waiting for them. The soldiers of both armies will work their way in and out of the houses as they advance through the town.

---

[196] Picture is from Oscar H. Darter 1957 Colonial Fredericksburg and Neighborhood In Perspective. P. 160. New York: Twayne Publishers.

Do you know how many bodies you would find when you returned to what was left of your home?

There would be one, two, three or more bodies which you will bury on your property.

The Broaddus home was no exception, when they returned to their home they found a dead Union Soldier in the hall way. They buried him in the back yard. Due to the extensive damage to the house The Broaddus Family was forced to move to Charlottesville. The later owners found that the ghost of the Union Soldier kept returning to the house.

One day a servant said she would lay him to rest and said a prayer over his grave – this should be the end of the story but it is not. There are still reports of sightings of figures in the house by different owners and visitors.

People see things in the garden at night which are not there during the day. We have been told of fire pits, mounds, and three soldiers in the garden.

Tenants in the dependency have heard foot steps at night and we have heard footsteps in the driveway. We had a man dressed in a blue uniform standing on the edge of the driveway he heard a voice say "get out". He turned to leave and footsteps followed him out of the driveway.

Another man dressed in a blue uniform was on the sidewalk on the opposite side of the driveway he was told to "hide".

We have had people hear the sound of the bayonet hitting gators as someone walked past. They see and hear Union Soldiers who speak with an Irish brogue. It is probably not the same man who is buried in the Broaddus garden. We do not know how many men are buried in this town.

1200 Block of Princess Anne Street

    This corner was the site of the first home of Fielding Lewis. In October of 1807 it was the home of Mr. Stannard who was laid out in state. The family was making cakes for his wake in the fireplace and somehow the roof caught on fire; they rescued Mr. Stannard's body by placing it in the garden.

    The fire burned forty-four blocks of town - jumped the river and burned part of the former Washington Family farm.

    In 1831 the mayor of the town, Robert Makey, built his home here at the cost of $30,000. The people of the town called it Mackey's Folly. The next owner was the Seddon Family one of their son's became our Secretary of War in the Confederacy. In 1850 this was the home of Thomas and Virginia Knox (who bore her tenth son in this house).

    In 1857 The Knox Family moved across the street to a house built in the 1790s, now known as the Kenmore Inn Bed and Breakfast. Here they had a total of ten boys and five girls. Mr. Knox was one of the men arrested by General Pope and sent to Capital Prison in Washington, D.C.[197]

---

[197] Both Pictures are From Hand colored Postcard Published by W. L. Bond, Druggist, Fredericksburg, Va. Post Cards of Quality.--The

1200 Princess Anne Street

On the second floor is Elizabeth's room. Elizabeth rearranges things. Where is the alarm clock? What happened to the book I was reading? Where is the toothpaste? Look under the bed, look in the closet, you will find the missing items in the room.

A family was sleeping here one night when the father was awakened by his daughter, who told him someone was playing with her hair she asked him to please trade beds.

He did as she asked and reported that no one had disturbed him during the night. When they inquired the next morning, a member of the staff told him, they have a ghost who plays with guest's hair. The reason that the father slept undisturbed was because he was bald.

A guest room on the front of the building had a four poster bed with a canopy and curtains. When you went to sleep the curtains were tied open. When you woke up the curtains were closed. You would find that the room had been cleaned and the curtain ties were lying in neat rows on the dresser. The management became weary of the guests complaining about the cleaning crew entering the room at night. They sold the furniture and the cleaning stopped.

Albertype Co Brooklyn, N. Y. (Bond's Drugstore was in Dr. Hall's Building pictured earlier).

A ghost named Anna appears to diners in the pub in the basement.

One morning, the cook was late for work, when he opened the kitchen door he heard the chef walking around kitchen. Then he heard the chef open the back door and leave.

This seemed to be unusual, so the cook followed the sounds, opened the back door to see where the chef was. He did not see the chef but he did see an undisturbed water puddle and no wet foot prints in or out. A few minutes later the chef actually arrived.

A man in 18th century clothing has been seen walking through the building. During a George Washington Birthday Celebration guests and staff were surprised to find pictures had been removed from the walls and lined up neatly on the floor.

This picture of Kenmore Bed and Breakfast has some mysterious figures. [198]

---

[198] Picture Taken by Chris Bloomquist

Lewis Street is named for Major Fielding Lewis, a great supporter of the Revolution and the husband of Betty Washington, George Washington's only surviving sister.

1200 Charles Street [199]

    The Mary Washington House was built as a gentleman's cottage and was purchased and improved by George Washington to provide a home for his mother. He brought her here in 1761. The wing to the right of the downspout was an addition placed by Rev. Wilson, a later owner of the house.

    This house seems to have a special blessing on its roof for every fire that has come through the town has turned the corner and not touched the house.

    In the 1890s the tenants were Robert and Mrs. Beale who accidentally overheard the owner discussing he was going to sell the house and send to the Chicago World's Fair. They reacted and helped to save it as a public property. Their overhearing and their reacting is a double blessing.

    In 1862 the home of Jane B. Beale, on the corner of Amelia and Charles Street, received major cannon damage

---

[199] Picture Taken by Theodor Horydczak (1890-1971) ca 1920-1950
This image is available online from the Library of Congress.

on the river side of the house and Kenmore Plantation three blocks up sustained cannon damage. Not a single cannon ball hit the Mary Washington House. During the War Between the States the owner of the house, Mrs. Dickenson, used the site as a hospital for the wounded soldiers.

A door on the second floor is very difficult to open. Meanwhile downstairs, in the parlor, there is a door that does not want to stay closed. While the docent is addressing a group, the door handle behind her will turn, the door will open, the door will swing closed, and the handle will turn.

People hear the sound of rustling of skirts.

During your visit, a docent will hold up a piece of soap and explain the life styles of the 18th century and return the soap to the soap stand. Later they find the soap has been moved to the other side of the stand or someone has taken the soap and pressed it into the holes.

There is a beautiful secretary with glass doors standing between the two front windows. While they are speaking with you, one of the docents may reach over and hold the door closed, or may even step back and lean against the door. This is to prevent the door from swinging open on its own accord – there have been occasions where the doors have swung open and the books have floated out.

The wing to the right of the drain pipe is believed to have been added after the death of Mary Washington by Reverend Samuel Wilson. We have seen a light come on at night through the dormer on the far right side - there are no light fixtures in the room.

One Christmas season, a volunteer was working in the basement of the annex during the evening. He had brought his radio to provide musical entertainment. The on and off switch no longer functioned in this radio so he would turn it off and on by plugging it into the wall. The tuning knob was also defective so the radio was set to one station.

He plugged in the radio and was listening to station that featured rock music. Suddenly the radio stopped playing. He checked to see if the plug had come out of the wall. The radio was not working and yet it was plugged in. He pulled the plug and reset it in the outlet, the radio came on and it played during the commercials, when the rock music started again the radio stopped.

When he finished his assignment he took the radio home, and plugged it in – the radio worked perfectly. It would seem that Rev Wilson, who had added that wing to the house, did not approve of his choice in music.

A picture of figures in the windows to the left of the door and a light in the window to the far right[200]

Mary Washington used to walk through the garden and travel three blocks more to visit her daughter, Betty Washington Lewis. People still see her walk through the garden and disappears at the garden gate. We have learned that she does not stop at gate, for she has been seen walking through people's houses.

---

[200] Picture Taken by Chris Bloomquist June 2004

Corner of Lewis and Charles Streets[201]

    The house on the corner of Lewis and Charles Streets was built in the 18th century by a son of Fielding and Betty Washington Lewis. It has served as a private residence, an inn, and an apartment complex for college students.
    Through time there have been haunting legends surrounding this house.
    The most enduring legend tells of a member of the Marine Corps who was renting this house for his family residence. His complaint to the land lord that the house was haunted and the ghost was scarring his children did not allow him to break the lease. The story continues that he went to his superiors and had the presence of a ghost certified by the Marine Corp.
    As one of the owners has stated, if this true, then this would seem to be the only house to have a ghost certified by the US Marine Corps.
    Charles Street is named for Charles of Orange who was the grandfather of William and Mary.

---

[201] Postcard Published by RA Kispaugh, Fredericksburg, VA. The Finest American Made View Post Cards, The Albertype Co. Brooklyn, N.Y.

307 Amelia Street [202]

The Presbyterian Church replaced their church building, located on this site, with The Female Orphan Asylum in 1834. An Asylum was a haven for young ladies where they were taught domestic skills so they could be self-sufficient.

The building had large rooms for dormitories and classrooms; which made it an ideal surgery - The floor boards became blood soaked. People tell us they see faces in the windows. Some people see a soldier standing in the door way. The most startling thing they will see is a dark figure forming next to the column on the Charles Street side of the porch. Some people also see another man in a cape standing below the edge of the porch.

After the War Between the States, Miss Rebekah Smith served here as the administrator of a home for gentle ladies the South - she was so loving and so kind they called the house The Smithsonia in her honor.[203]

Following Miss Smith, the church used the building as a college until1917, when due to a financial difficulties, it was sold as a private residence.

Over time, the building deteriorated greatly. Several years ago, a family purchased the house and performed a

---

[202] Picture Taken by Author
[203] Miss Rebekah Smith was the sister of James Powers Smith who was the Minister of the Presbyterian Church.

three year restoration including a copper topped gazebo; an atrium; and an elevator which has made it into a fine Southern home.

Here are two pictures of the Smithsonia showing a mysterious cloud figure.[204]

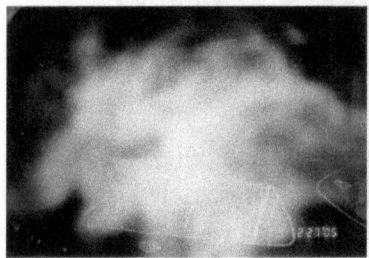

---
[204] Pictures Taken by Teresa and Sara Auth, October 2005

These two pictures include a figure on the porch by the third column and a light in the window. There may be a figure on the upper bench on the left; and in both pictures there is a strange figure and a glow.[205]

---

[205] Picture Taken by Chris Bloomquist June 2004

1016 Charles Street[206]

    The bank on the corner of Charles Amelia Streets was the site of the office of Bridgewater Mills, who had a milling operation on the Rappahannock River. The first commercial phone line in the Commonwealth of Virginia was stretched from this site to the mill.

    Bridgewater Mills received a prize in 1878 at a Paris Exposition for their fine grained flour.

    The Ficklin Family owned both the mill and Rappahannock Light and Power Company. Mrs. Ficklin was the first woman in the country to actually run a utility. She held the position from 1900 to 1923.

    The bank may be haunted. One evening as we were passing the bank, the lights were flashing on the right end, and the letter box kept opening and closing.

    Some of us thought the cleaning crew was responsible for this and we moved on to our next destination. A member of our party crept back to find that the lights were still flashing and letter drop was still opening and closing. The next day we learned from the bank staff that they had often experienced unexplained doors opening and closing and had seen the lights flickering.

---

[206] Picture Taken by Author

This site, like the Mary Washington House, may have a special protection surrounding it. When the plans were finalized for the construction of this building there was a house on the site that needed to be demolished.

The method of demolition, at that time, was to drive a bull dozer into the walls of the house and have it cave in upon itself and then remove the debris.

Things did not go as planned on the day of destruction, for when the bulldozer impacted on the house instead of the pieces falling in – the house came down upon the bulldozer and the driver.

His relatives still tell the story of how the house fell down around him and he walked out without a single scratch.

William Street is named for William, the Son of King George 2nd, he is the man who introduced the Ascot Races to England. The street is also known as Plank Road, a name that dates from 1850, when the merchants in town laid planks eight feet long and four feet wide on the incoming side of the road so their merchandise could be brought into town

Corner of Charles and William Streets[207]

---

[207] Picture from a Postcard with Copyright by by R. A. Kishpaugh, Fredericksburg, VA. Genuine Curteich-Chicago "C.T. American Ar" Post Card (Reg. U.S. Pat. Off.)

On this intersection stands the slave auction block in front of the U. S. Hotel erected in 1851. After we separated from the Union the name was changed to Planter's Hotel.

Following the War Between the States, it was purchased by two of the Knox Brothers[208] who changed the name to the Knoxanna Building and converted it to shops and offices.

A picture of orbs and clouds on the corner.[209]

900 Block of Charles Street[210]

---
[208] Picture Taken by Teresa and Sara Auth, October 2005
[209] These are two of the ten sons of the Knox Family on Princess Anne Street

James Monroe was the 5th President of the United States. He came to Fredericksburg at the request of his uncle. While here he was elected to city council; by the time Mr. Monroe died he had held more offices than anyone in the country.

James Monroe died on the 4th of July 1831. When he died, his descendents gathered everything he owned to be protected until a museum could be opened in his honor. [211]

The James Monroe Museum was not opened until 1927. What a special man he must have been to influence his descendents to hold onto everything he owned for almost one hundred years

The museum is haunted. The most famous haunting story takes place on a snowy day in December of 1927. The last descendant, Mr. Hoes, was walking from the Masonic cemetery toward the front door.

In the distance he saw two men outside the door of the building. One was very tall and had red hair, the other is shorter with dark hair. Mr. Hoes will not loose a dollar in admission fees, so he shouted to the men: "the door is open you may go in". They did not react.

As he traveled closer to the building he was surprised to see that they were wearing 18th century clothing, something you did not see very often in 1927. He hollered one more time. This time they reacted, they waved to him, and went inside the building.

---

[210] Picture Taken by Theodor Horydczak (1890-1971) ca 1920-1950 This image is available online from the Library of Congress
[211] Picture of James Monroe's Grave in 1905 is entitled "2585 G" on negative. Detroit Publishing Co. no. 018418. in the Library of Congress Detroit Publishing Company Print Collection available online.

Mr. Hoes ran to the door and discovered it was locked! He pounded on the door demanding admission. Finally, one of the guides came and unlocked the door. No one had come in, and no one had locked the door. The door had changed. There were now large vertical cracks in the door. It is believed he saw Jefferson and Monroe. Could they have gone through the door instead of entering it?

The cracks were repaired many times over the next few years and every time they returned. The museum determined it was best to replace the door with another one. We have stood outside the door and heard knockings from within. We have seen the chandelier sway from side to side.

There is a rumored story of an event that took place one afternoon in the building. It would seem that one of the staff members had her teen age daughter and a friend upstairs between school and closing time. They were responsible, reliable, young ladies. Since the staff member needed to stay late, she instructed the girls to wait for her while she went out to get a pizza.

They were sitting in the office upstairs reading in their stocking feet; when suddenly an alarm went off in the building. They put on their shoes and looked to see what had happened.

The police came and the mother returned with the pizza. She was allowed to take the girls out to her car.

"Did you, at any time, go out and walk through the garden?" She asked.

"No, remember we had our shoes off and you asked us to wait in the office".

"The reason I asked is because the police found muddy footprints in the hallway downstairs."

The blinds in the dormers move at night. They swing from side to side or back to front. We have actually had evenings where we have seen the blinds opening and closing. One of the windows is an attic storage area - there is no heat or air conditioning which could cause the blinds to move.

The top picture has a figure in the dormer. The one to the right has some orbs and some people see a figure in the dormer. [212]

There is a figure in the dormer in the picture on the left and the blinds are being separated by someone or something. In the picture on the right there may be a figure

---

[212] Pictures Taken by Beverly Amberg September 1998

in the dormer and there is a light in the window on the first floor.[213]

The top picture is of the dormer at night with a possible figure in the window. The other three were taken during the day showing figures on and around the building.

---

[213] Pictures Taken by Anonymous Donors

The second & third pictures show a figure to the right of the door and additional figures. The fourth picture also shows the Masonic Cemetery with a figure on the wall.[214]

This picture shows a figure in the dormer and many people contend that that they can see through the people on the left.[215]

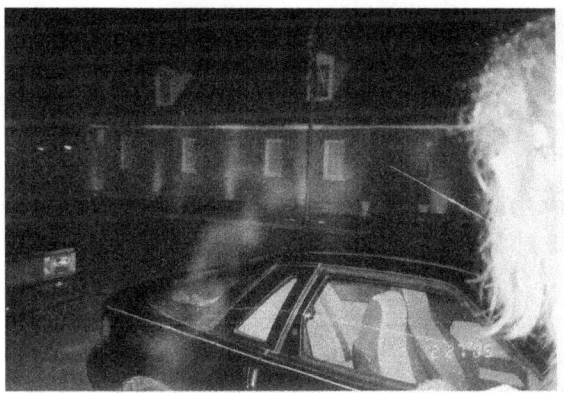

---

[214] Pictures Taken by Michael Matthieu
[215] Picture Taken by Dylan Waugh October 1996

A picture of a possible figure in the dormer and a figure forming on the street[216]

*Masonic Cemetery
Corner of Charles and George Streets*[217]

The Masonic Cemetery is believed to be the oldest Masonic Cemetery in the country originating in 1784. The walls bear cannon strikes from the shelling of the town in 1862.

The first American to make a million dollars in cash, Basil Gordon, is buried here. He was fortunate enough to have an agent in England at the right moment to make a large [218]tobacco trade just before the market would drop.

Inside the gate, is the large red tombstone of John Minor and Lucy Landon Carter. John Minor born in 1761 at the age of fourteen, became

---

[216] Picture Taken by Teresa and Sara Auth October 2005
[217] Picture is an 1881stereoptican image in possession of Historic Fredericksburg Foundation, Inc. Published on URL: http://departments.umw.edu/hipr/www/Fredericksburg/1881pics.htm
[218] Picture Taken by Author

known as the Boy General of the Revolution. At the age of twenty he wrote the first Emancipation Proclamation.

On June the 8th, 1816 General Minor was speaking at a General Assembly Dinner in Richmond, Virginia. At precisely 6 PM his wife, six of the seven children, and the tutor were all having dinner in his home south of town, Hazel Hill.[219]

The servant opened the dining room door and asked, "Do you know the Master has come home?"

Lucy answered "No, but we all want to see him."

They ran out in the foyer and there he was in full evening dress. He looked at his family and went up the stairs. They could clearly see his hands and the ruffles on his sleeves. The children loved their father so very much that they followed him up the stairs. They could not find him anywhere in the house.

That same evening there was a family gathering at John Minor's boy hood home, Topping Castle, in King George County. Some of the family members came downstairs to report that "John Minor is upstairs"

It was not until many hours later, a horse came from Richmond, with the rider bearing the news, the General had died at 6 PM at dinner.

His wife, Lucy, refused to ever have the incident mentioned in her presence - she sold Hazel Hill and moved to a house on lower Caroline Street.[220]

---

[219] This picture appeared in Oscar H. Darter 1957 Colonial Fredericksburg and Neighborhood In Perspective. P. 154. New York: Twayne Publishers and was provided Courtesy Sidney J. Shannon Jr., present owner. The house stood at the end of Princess Anne Street across from George Washington's Boyhood Home.

John Minor's daughter, Mary Berkley Minor, married William Matthews Blackford; a man of many talents. He was an inventor, an attorney, newspaper editor, diplomat to Columbia, and a banker. They had seven children: Lucy, Isabella, Charles, Eugene, William, Lancelot and Lewis.

A block from the cemetery was the home of William DeBaptiste, a shipping merchant who is a free black.

Fredericksburg had indentured servants and slaves. The majority of the slave trade was on the river and on Wolfe Street. There was also the Monrovia movement - where you freed the slave, you trained him and then sent him to Africa so he can remain free and self-sufficient.

Mary Minor Blackford was key leader of the Monrovia movement, working to rescue these people from their situation. Her sons became officers in the Confederacy serving with different units. They returned to serve on Marye's Heights in 1862 during the Battle of Fredericksburg.

After the conflict, the Blackford boys came into town and checked on their grandfather's grave, which still bears bullet strikes.[221] Then they returned to the house of their childhood, passing on the way, homes of

---

[220] Picture is from Oscar H. Darter 1957 Colonial Fredericksburg and Neighborhood In Perspective. P.146 New York: Twayne Publishers. The original caption reads Courtesy of Mrs. W. W. Braxton.

[221] Picture Taken by Author

friends and relatives, noting the destruction of familiar places. Upon arriving at their home, they discovered damage from a cannon ball which passed through the dependency.

They found the body of a Union Soldier in the fan light window of the room they had used as a nursery and buried him by the mulberry tree in the back yard.

The Blackford Boys used their old home place as a temporary headquarters. This family is living proof that the issue of the war in the South was state's rights and not slavery.

It must be noted, when Mr. Lincoln introduced the Emancipation Proclamation, the Union Army found that many of their soldiers deserted. They said they were not fighting over slavery they were fighting for the preservation of the union.

Slavery was an evil in both the North and the South. The underground railroad took those seeking freedom to Canada, because the slavery in the North was equal too, or worse than, the slavery in the South.

The 1860 Census of Fredericksburg shows the population consisted of four thousand "whites and free blacks." The citizenry had whites, free blacks, slaves, indentures, and the Monrovia movement, all in the same town at the same time.

The cemetery has been a scene of haunting experiences for many people.

One evening, one of our guests requested that we cross to the other side of Charles Street, because she saw a Funeral Procession going into the cemetery and she did not want us to interfere with them.

Lewis Littlepage, of Hanover County, Virginia; was a General during the Revolution, and then traveled to Europe where he became a confidant of the King of Poland.

In October of 1801 he returned to Virginia where he died on July 19th, 1802. His will divided his estate among his siblings and their children.

Lewis Littlepage's brother used his inheritance to purchase a large piece of acreage and build a home now lovingly maintained as the Littlepage Inn.

We were contracted to entertain the guests for a wedding party staying at the Littlepage Inn during the day of the wedding being held on July19th - which was also the date of the General's death.

General Littepage was buried in the Masonic Cemetery. We determined that we should perform a small ceremony by his grave to honor him and to recognize the beginning of a new life for a special couple.

To accomplish this, we would need to know where his grave was located. A few days before the event, a member of our company walked through the cemetery gates, went past the grave of General John Minor and looked to the right. There was a group of people dressed n black standing in a circle.

"That must be it"

When she walked in that direction the people were gone, and where they had been standing, was the grave of Lewis Littlepage.

Mr. Barlious was a confectioner in Fredericksburg. He developed an illness that lasted about three years. During this illness, he strongly instructed his wife, she was to make sure he was really dead before she buried him.

When he died, he was laid in state for three days and then they buried him in the Masonic Cemetery. The grave cannot be found.

One of the greatest fears of the 18th and 19th century was the possibility of being buried alive. We would try to make sure that a person was really deceased before we would place them in a grave.

One method was to have them lie in state for a several days with people watching the body in case the individual would awaken. Another method was to hold a mirror under the deceased person's nose to detect any breathing.

We also had a device invented by Mr. Batson called Batson's Belfry. This was a small spire containing a bell with a rope attached. The string or rope was tied to the wrist of the deceased individual and when the burial took place the bell was placed on the ground by the grave. If you woke up in the casket your arms would move and the bell would ring.

We hired people to work on the graveyard shift, to listen for whom the bell tolled; and if the bell did ring they would come and open the grave and save your life.

At night, when the cemetery is closed, people will come up to the gate and they will look in and then step back because there is something inside the gate. We have had incidents where people have felt someone come past them through the gates.

Others have leaned against the pillars by the gate, and felt a distinct movement of the wall behind them.

Pictures of lights and orbs in the cemetery[222]

---

[222] Picture on left Taken by Beverly Amberg, September 1998
Picture on right Taken by Chris Bloomquist, June 2004

Two pictures of the grave of John Minor with figures, orbs, and lights[223]

A mysterious cloud forming around the Cemetery gate [224]

---

[223] Both Pictures Taken by Kelly Doyle May 2002
[224] Picture Taken by Teresa and Sara Auth October 2005;

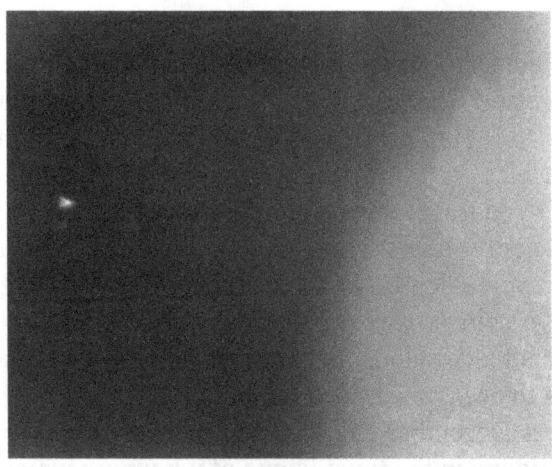

This picture shows a light, and a figure to the right, by the bush, just inside of the cemetery gate. [225]

We have no streets named for George Washington. George Street is named in honor of King George.

George Street Intersecting With Charles Street[226]

---

[225] Picture Taken by Michael Matthieu
[226] [226] Picture is an 1881 stereoptican image in possession of Historic Fredericksburg Foundation, Inc. Published on URL: http://departments.umw.edu/hipr/www/Fredericksburg/1881pics.htm
This picture shows the Methodist Church South which looked very much like the Presbyterian Church.

One October night, we finished a walk on the corner of George and Charles Streets by telling the story of Col. Cross of New Hampshire and we got a bonus haunting experience.

If you travel down George Street you will find the canal. Where soldiers would have to lay planks under fire or swim in twelve degree water to assault Marye's Heights.

One block over, on the corner of Charles and Hanover Streets, stands the home of Montgomery Slaughter, who was the Mayor of the town in 1862.

It is December 13, 1862 and there are about 100,000 Union soldiers in the town (some of whom are women dressed as men).

The first three waves assaulted Marye's heights fixed bayonets only, the next wave had munitions. As they marched forward there were walking wounded coming toward them and litter bearers carrying the wounded all around the advancing soldiers.

The houses on the street on both sides are all surgeries, as the soldiers passed they heard their fellow soldiers screaming in pain - and they saw the limbs flying out of the windows.

As they continued the march toward the Heights the wounded and dying pulled on their pant legs begging them not to go.

One block over, and farther up, on Hanover Street lied Col. Cross of New Hampshire, who was wounded. His fellow soldiers did not see him. They marched past him and over him some of them accidentally stepping on his body.

Finally someone found him and brought him back to the home of Mayor Slaughter which was now a surgery.

The Surgeon took one look at Col. Cross and stated "This man is dead throw his body out"

Col. Cross screamed: "I am not dead!"

They did operate on him; he survived and joined the Battle of Chancellorsville with an unhealed wound.

After Chancellorsville, Col. Cross was in Gettysburg where he was informed that after this battle he would receive a promotion.

He told them he was not going to receive a promotion instead was going to die in this battle. In preparation for this event, he dressed himself in black and he did die, that day on the wheat field.

In Fredericksburg, on the day after the battle, there were children soldiers who recounted that outside of every house there were piles of limbs and there were also piles of bodies. Those piles were groaning because there were live men buried in them.[227]

This particular evening, I gestured toward the Masonic Cemetery, and said: "Col. Cross could have wound up buried somewhere in the town".

---

[227] This picture of a burial party on Charles Street was taken May 1863 by Timothy H. O'Sullivan (1840-1882). Is available online through the Library of Congress.

A member of the group, who had been leaning against the brick wall by the parking lot, said in a very deep voice "He was a Mason you know."

I said "Who?"

"Col. Cross" he replied in an unusually deep voice

"Thank you - interesting tone of voice." I replied

The group began to break up, and members of the party, asked the man how he knew Col. Cross was a Mason. He looked at us and said: "What are you talking about?" Several people separately told him that you stood right over there and said; "He was a Mason".

The man looked at each one and told them he had said nothing. It was even more unique because his tone of was not as deep as the one he used when he made the statement. He did some research on Col. Cross and learned that he had been a member of the Masonic Order.

Federal Hill[228]

Federal Hill was built about 1790 by the third Governor of Virginia, Robert Brooke, who was a member of the Federalist Party. The three story house, with a full basement and an attic, was rumored for many years to

---

[228] Hand Colored Postcard Published by W.L. Bond, Druggist, Fredericksburg, Va. Post Cards of Quality The Albertype Co., Brooklyn, N.Y.

haunted by Lt. Governor Alexander Spottswood of Virginia, (for whom Spotsylvania County is named).

Alexander Spottswood (1676 -1740); became a Major General in the British Army, served as Lt Governor of Virginia where he erected the first iron furnace in North America; and led expeditions into the Shenandoah Valley of Virginia. While Lt. Governor Spottswood would become related through cousins to the Washington & Lee Families there do not seem to be any established links to Federal Hill, to the property, nor the owner, during the time period of construction in the 1790s.

One of the early 20th century residents noted that when she would be sitting at her writing desk someone would touch her arm.

A more recent resident of Federal Hill did not experience appearances of Governor Spottswood but did notice that the doors of the sideboard in the dining room would many times be found open; the door bell would ring at different times of the day, sometimes while you were standing in the entry hall with the outside doors open.

In 1862 the house stood on the edge of town, looking across the open fields on each side of the canal and up onto the ridge which became the site of the great confrontation between the Union and Confederate armies.

The owner of Federal Hill, before the conflict between the North and the South, was Thomas Reede Roots whose daughter married into the Cobb Family of Georgia. To this union was born two sons named Howell Cobb and Thomas Reede Roots Cobb.

Every summer she would bring the boys to the home of their grandparents where they would play in the fields and knew the town as a second home.

In December of 1862, Thomas RR Cobb returned to Fredericksburg, serving as the General of Cobb's Legion an Irish unit from Georgia. They are positioned on Marye's Heights across from Federal Hill, near the homes of the Innis

Family and Martha Stevens. So his men can better see him and hear his commands, General Cobb is on horse back, in the Sunken Road.

The home of his grandfather is occupied by the Union Army.

Thomas RR Cobb was killed within site of the house he played in as a child.

There are conflicting versions of the story of how General Cobb died. While one version states he was taken down by a sharpshooter; there is a Cobb family legend which states it more eloquently.

Many years after the death of General Cobb, a member of the United States Senate and his family was taken through Federal Hill by the owner.

When they approached the parlor a female member of the party suddenly sat down on the couch and said "I am sorry I cannot go on."

The senator turned to his hostess and explained: "Please forgive my wife, she is the daughter of Thomas RR Cobb and I feel the emotion is too great for her. You see her family believes he was killed by a cannon placed in front of the window where he and his wife had married in that room."

The room he was referring to did have the remains of a small cannon lunette in front of the far window.

A picture toward Marye's Heights taken from Federal Hill showing is a distinct face in the center.[229]

The area of the Battle of Fredericksburg, known as Prospect Hill, and the house still known as Mansfield, were the scenes of much blood shed and sorrow and they do have many haunting stories.

Braehead, still stands in the center section of the Battlefield. The house was built by John Howison and then transferred to his brother Robert Reid Howison and still bears some of the scars from the assaults of the Union Army. One of the Howison descendants was a Park Ranger who preserved the site of the battle by donating his land to the Park Service.

Marye's Heights, was the scene of much sorrow and pain. The one story we will share here with a ghost picture is of Martha Stevens.

Martha Stevens house stood on the Sunken Road and even though she saw the Confederate Army gather outside her door she would not leave her home; some accounts say she was alone, while others state she had servants with her.

When the assault on Marye's Heights takes place "Granny Stevens" house becomes riddled with bullets and she is not personally injured.

It is recorded that this woman will rescue either personally, or through her servants, wounded men from both sides of the conflict. She will provide them with water and she will rip her clothing to make bandages for their wounds.

Many people tell her story in the form of a joke because after the conflict she was embarrassed to meet Confederate Officers with her petticoats missing.

It is not a laughing matter, for in the 19th century women wear certain, specific layers, of clothing. If lady appears in public with out the layers, the clothing hangs

---

[229] Picture Taken by Author

improperly and people will know, by her appearance, she is not properly attired.

By virtue of tearing her petticoats to make bandages for men she did not even know - Martha Stevens risked her reputation as a virtuous woman and she was painfully aware and embarrassed by having people see her appear dressed as an improper woman.

The Martha Stevens House no longer stands on Marye's Heights. This picture was taken in August of 1970 and shows a figure in the window. Some people see figures on the house and in the other windows.[230]

---

[230] Picture Taken by Clarence G. Anespake Jr. August 1970

1200 Charles Street [231]

The Rising Sun Tavern, built as a residence in 1760, was originally the private home of Charles Washington the brother of George Washington; who sold the property to move farther west.

A later owner will convert the house to a public, proper tavern. Despite the fires in the tow; floods, the war of independence, the shelling of the town in 1862, and the frequent change of ownership, much of the building still contains the original materials

Today it is a public property. where they explain the life style, foods and expressions of the time.

One of the tavern keepers was a Mr. Frazier, who is believed to haunt the building. Mr. Frazier will tug at lady's skirts on the stairway or will remove men's hats.

---

[231] Picture Published by Fredericksburg News Agency. "Tichnor Quality Views" Reg. U.S. Pat. Office. Made only by Tichnor Bros. Inc, Boston, Mass.

These two pictures captured orbs and lights on the porch and on the roof.[232]

---

[232] Pictures taken by Denise Bryant

Kenmore Plantation[233]

The house now known as Kenmore Plantation was built before the American Revolution by Fielding Lewis who was married to George Washington's only surviving sister.

Mr. Lewis hired the stucco man from Mt Vernon to trim the ceilings and mantles of rooms on the first floor. The mantle in the dining room still bears the scenes from an Aesop fable suggested by George Washington.

Fielding Lewis supported the Revolution, he built ships; he manufactured weapons; he gave all he had – and he lost every penny to the cause. The night that he learned of the Cornwallis surrender Fielding Lewis died from the financial distress.

When Betty Washington Lewis died the house was sold at auction to pay the debts incurred to buy our freedom.

People will see Fielding Lewis walking the grounds looking worried. Many people have seen him sitting at the desk in his bedroom studying his books in great distress.

The house, like so many others, will serve as a surgery during the Union occupations and invasions of the

---

[233] Postcard Published by Kenmore Association, Fredericksburg, VA. Post Cards of Quality –The Albertype Co., Brooklyn, N.Y.

town. People have seen soldiers in the house and on the grounds.

One night after a presentation, given for descendants of Gordon Family, who were the owners of the house in the 19th century - a member of our staff felt a cold presence and he met Fielding Lewis in the foyer of the house.

The carriage entrance door is attached to a security alarm, nevertheless, it will be found hanging open at night. The police will come and search the house, close the door, only to have to return later; because it has reopened.

They also have the opposite problem; where the door refuses to be opened. They will try to unlock the door and open it from the outside - and the only way it will swing open is if someone goes inside and pulls it open.

We have had people see lights and figures in the windows at night and they have also seen a figure in black step off of the door.

This picture shows an image on the door and some orbs and lights; some people see figures on each side of the door. [234]

---

[234] Picture Taken by Beverly Amberg

Here we have a series of ghost pictures taken on our walk of places that we cannot identify[235]

---
[235] Top left Picture Taken by Nick Ieardi ; The two center Pictures Taken by Sara and Teresa Auth October 2005; The last Picture Taken by Anonymous Donor

We sincerely hope you have enjoyed your journey through history and that you will always remember and honor those who have preceded you.

www.ingramcontent.com/pod-product-compliance
Lightning Source LLC
Chambersburg PA
CBHW050638160426
43194CB00010B/1719